Buying and Reschooling
Ex-Racehorses

is to be returned on or before
st date stamped below.

BUYING *and* RESCHOOLING EX~RACEHORSES

Christopher and Victoria Coldrey

The Crowood Press

First Published in 1997 by
The Crowood Press Ltd
Ramsbury, Marlborough
Wiltshire SN8 2HR

British Library Cataloguing-in-Publication Data

A catalogue record for this book is available from the British Library.

ISBN 1 86126 088 1

Dedication
This book is dedicated to the hundreds of volunteers of the British Horse Society who give their time so generously and unstintingly to ensure the welfare and good management of our horses and ponies in these islands.

Authors' Note
For easy reading and to keep the text simple throughout, the word 'man' (as, for example, in 'horseman') means mankind and includes both sexes. Similarly we refer to horses throughout as 'he', meaning either sex, to avoid talking about a horse as 'it', which turns him into an object and not a sentient being.

Photographs by Chistopher Coldrey, except where stated otherwise.
Line-drawings by Sara Wyche, except those on pages 107-108, which are by Matthew Lawrence
Typeset by Phoenix Typesetting, Ilkley, West Yorkshire.
Printed and bound in Great Britain by WBC Book Manufacturers Ltd, Mid Glamorgan

Contents

Acknowledgements

Our special thanks go to the team who co-operated in the reschooling of the two 'guinea-pig' horses, Gondolier and Rare Melody. We are indeed lucky to have people of such understanding and ability on our staff. It was Emma Haigh, Bizzie Budden, Kate Hodgkins, Annette Robson and Catharina Sonsthagen (Norway) who were so patient, not only working the horses so successfully but doing it while dodging the photographer.

We are extremely grateful to Lord Howard de Walden and his racing manager, Leslie Harrison, and to Caroline Schweir for lending us their lovely horses. They were ideal subjects, completely different from one another, yet both thrilling to work with.

Special thanks to Lindsay Boggie, our secretary, who battled with some dreadful and much-altered and crossed-out hand-writing to produce a readable typescript.

The contributions from Sarah Culverwell (physiotherapy) and Stephen Gowing A.W.C.F. (feet) add important extras for the buyers of ex-racehorses.

The cartoons were drawn by Charles Murray-Brown. He is really a busy architect in Edinburgh but, having seen similar work to these, I was luckily able to prevail upon him to add these witty touches to *Buying and Reschooling Ex-Racehorses*.

Sue Montgomery, who is a mine of information, helped us with the details concerning event horses. It makes life easy when there are experts available with help and information.

All the photographs for the book were taken by Christopher Coldrey except those with special credits. We are very grateful for permission to use these pictures.

Foreword

In asking me to write a foreword to this book the authors have paid me a great compliment. It is a first for me and I think it is also a first for a book on this important subject.

The book touches upon all aspects of horsemanship by explaining most clearly and concisely how to go about taking a Thoroughbred future competition horse from the racehorses that become available each year, and how to go about converting him to your purposes through loose schooling.

To acquire a horse with perfect conformation would be extremely lucky to say the least, for such a horse must be one in a million. But this book is a guideline for those seeking the best: it shows you how to recognize it when you see it, and how to make the most of your ex-racehorse's attributes.

In writing this book, the authors offer their wealth of practical experience, explaining the retraining methods that will give your horse every chance of enjoying a useful and successful life now that his racing career is at an end.

Any training is all about understanding the horse's mind. Every horse needs a different approach, and the art is knowing when to be patient and when to demand more. It is an art that can be learned, and from this book there is a great deal to learn. It doesn't happen overnight, but learning to train a horse well can be an intensely rewarding experience. And in educating the human, this book will give the ex-racehorse a better chance of finding a new and successful career.

Kristina Gifford, 1997.

Introduction

We wanted to call this book 'No ! We don't shoot horses'. But it was thought that too few people would recognize the allusion to a UK Channel 4 TV programme called *They Shoot Horses Don't They*? It castigated racehorse owners who send their retiring horses to auction and don't, thereafter, know what becomes of them. Occasionally, and inevitably, a good and faithful horse falls on hard times and there is, rightly, an outcry about it. Here, we are trying to show that there are already top-notch competition horses who started on the racecourse, that there is an endless supply of such horses, and that the conversion from racehorse to competition horse need not be complicated or difficult: the methods we describe provide a good way of introducing them to a new, useful and happy life.

Victoria Coldrey on Bevendean at the Holcombe Hunt Point to Point. After racing, Bevendean was bought by John Greenwood who took her to Grade A showjumping under the name of Sky Fly. Sky Fly was influential in launching his daughter Gillian's international showjumping career.

When I lived in Southern Africa during the 1960s nearly all good competition horses were Thoroughbreds and most of them came off the racecourse. I bought quite a number of them, reschooled them, started them off on a showjumping career and sold them on.

The system that we used then is fundamentally the one described in this book. I was lucky to have a great character called Mike to help me. He was a Zulu who had an engaging affinity with horses and became brilliant at training them in the loose school. They were not ridden for at least six weeks after we started working them loose. By that time they were obedient to the voice – 'Walk', 'Trot', 'Canter', 'Change' (the rein), 'Stand' and 'Come here'. They were jumping single fences, doubles and gymnastic exercises with style and enjoyment. We had some very difficult horses wished upon us and all of them ended up by bringing pleasure to themselves and their new owners.

In Zimbabwe (or Rhodesia as it was then), I was rung up by a trainer (an Irishman of considerable wit and charm) saying that he had a horse called Fancy Rio that I might be interested in. She belonged to Lord Acton and had been warned off the racecourse for refusing to start; I could have her for £30. This was very cheap even that long ago. The upshot was that I bought her, reschooled her, and rode her many times in the Rhodesian Showjumping Team. She was, in fact, in the only Rhodesian team ever to beat the mighty South Africans. I eventually sold her to a very good young rider in South Africa. Thirty years later I met Lord Acton's son, Robert, who immediately said 'Oh yes, I remember my father gave you a horse in Rhodesia.' 'No,' I replied, 'he sold me a horse.' 'Well,' he said, 'I'm certain he told the trainer to give her to you . . .'

The growth of the relationship between you and your horse in the loose school is utterly enthralling. From the start, when there is suspicion or distrust or uncertainty, the bonding develops into such a

Christopher Coldrey on Pinto at the CS10 in Rome 1956.

9

rapport that words become unnecessary and the tiniest movement is sufficient for your partner to respond. Describing this later on, we call it a dance; indeed when Mike went out to a paddock to fetch horses he used, literally, to dance with them. It was lovely to watch the pair of them enjoying themselves as they circled one another, halted, stepped sideways and came together in a routine that was an unselfconscious demonstration of mutual affection and trust.

During the period of loose work you will see the traumas disappear from even the most uptight of ex-racehorses as they relax and enjoy their new challenges. Many of them are already completely self-assured and at ease with themselves, like Gondolier (whose progress is mapped in this book). But others, like Rare Melody (whom you will also meet), are full of apprehension and misgivings and it is these that are often the most rewarding in the end.

In recent times a mystique has grown up around people described as 'horse whisperers' or 'those who talk to horses' and the like. While there are, indeed, people who are especially gifted with animals – including horses – I am anxious to explain that bonding, establishing rapport with your horse, using effective body language, making your horse feel good and at ease with life, requires nothing more than sensitivity, application and common sense. Doctor Doolittle did not use magic; he used common sense and credited animals with more intelligence than it was normal to do in Hugh Lofting's time.

Today we realize that animals can reason, feel contented or miserable, love or fear people, try hard to please, enjoy affection and praise. When you understand that you will be a more successful trainer of horses as well as deriving more pleasure from your work.

It isn't magic that you need. It is understanding and a hefty dose of common sense.

1 The Source

What becomes of the huge numbers of horses that go out of racing each year? In the United Kingdom and Ireland there are some 15,000 horses in training. Since these are mostly between two and four years old it follows that between four and five thousand of them finish racing every year.

Of these:

• Some are sold to continue their racing careers in other countries where the standard of performance is not so high;
• Some flat racehorses that are suitable go on to national hunt racing;
• Some that are chronically unsound are humanely destroyed;
• The best colts are retained or sold to become stallions;
• The best fillies are retained or sold to go to stud as brood-mares;
• Some are bought at sales by knowledgeable people to become eventers, showjumpers, all-round competition horses, or riding horses;
• Some fall into unsuitable hands, fail to convert to the use for which they were bought, are sold again, maybe several times, and sink steadily down the ladder.

It is this last category of horses that people rightly worry about. Very occasionally it happens to a once-famous horse and when it is discovered there is a national outcry. But it is just as disgraceful if the humblest of horses ends his days in neglect, thirst, hunger, pain. To save a horse from this, which is often the result as much of ignorance as of wilful abuse, is a fine objective, and just sometimes the result can be sheer magic.

Witness the case of a glorious Arab colt that was given to the King of France by the Bey of Tunis in about 1730. The King gave him away to his chef and the downward spiral started. It is said that eventually this noble horse, in dreadful condition, was reduced to pulling a water cart through the streets of Paris. In any case, he was in very poor condition indeed when a certain Mr Edward Coke, an Englishman, saw the wretched animal, recognized the beauty beneath the neglect, and bought him.

Soon after returning to England he sold the horse to Lord Godolphin. Almost three centuries later, the Godolphin Arabian is still a household name. One of three Arabian horses that are the progenitors of the modern racehorse, Sham (pronounced to rhyme with 'harm'), is a direct ancestor of the great American stallion, Man O' War, and of about a third of all Thoroughbred horses alive today. It is interesting that the world's current leading owner of racehorses, Sheikh Mohammed Al Maktoum, has named his chief racing interest 'Godolphin' after the English nobleman whose horse has had such influence on the sport of kings.

The Goldophin Arabian: the legend and, below, the reality as depicted by Stubbs.

But it was only by pure chance that this noble beast did not die of poverty and neglect in the streets and stews of Paris. As it was, he died at the ripe old age of twenty-nine, full of years and honour, at Lord Godolphin's Cambridgeshire stud, Gog-magog.

There is also a story that the Godolphin Arabian started his career at Gog-magog stud as a teaser for a stallion called Hobgoblin. Hobgoblin was due to cover a mare called Roxana when Sham broke away from his handler, attacked and drove off Hobgoblin, and covered the mare himself. From this union came a colt called Cade, who continued the male line which produced great horses like Matchem, Hurry On, Precipitation, Santa Claus and Man O'War. Known as the 'Matchem Line' the descendants of Sham have played a huge part on both sides of the Atlantic for more than 200 years.

Alas, these tales turn out to be myths and are debunked, with charm, by Mordaunt Milner in his book, *The Godolphin Arabian: the story of the Matchem Line* (*see* Bibliography). Sham is described as a dark bay horse of great beauty with a wild, haughty appearance. Vicomte de Manty, who saw him when he was in France, says of him:

> He was of beautiful conformation, exquisitely proportioned with large hocks, well let down, with legs of iron . . . a horse of incomparable beauty whose only flaw was being headstrong.

So the story of his attack on Hobgoblin could be true; and if he was so difficult he might have been given away, for the Vicomte also wrote that the horse was . . .

in poor condition and very thin, and, though put in the Royal Stables, was despised and neglected and the grooms disliked him because he was quick and fiery and hard to ride.

The other two ancestors of the modern Thoroughbred are the Darley Arabian and the Byerley Turk. There were other imports of stallions from the Middle East, but their male lines have died out, leaving these three super-sires. Many of these horses have romantic stories. The Cullen Arabian was presented to the British Consul by the Emperor of Morocco and was later brought to England where he became the property of Lord Cullen and a famous sire of racehorses in the middle of the eighteenth century.

The passion for European warmblooded horses that has swept the English-speaking world in recent years has tended to blind us to the enormous amount of wonderful Thoroughbred material available to us.

In the 1980s American and Canadian showjumpers inexplicably moved away from the glorious, big, scopey Thoroughbreds on which they had conquered the world time after time, in favour of European Warmbloods. Since then they have ceased to be the irresistible force they had become, handing back that title to the Germans. Ideally suited in style to these powerful and obedient animals, the Germans have led the showjumping world virtually since the Second World War, except for a period of American interregnum and some glorious purple patches of British success. I remember I was building courses at the Loblaw's Classic in Toronto. A very good Canadian showjumper, Nancy Wetmore, who had made this change from Thoroughbred to Warmblood, took a nasty fall at a big treble combination. I rushed anxiously across the arena, 'Nancy! Are you all right?'

'You know why the Germans were late for the battle of Waterloo?' she asked. I thought she must be concussed. 'Because they were riding b— Hanoverians!'

I well remember a brilliant talk by Seamus Hayes, the great Irish show-jumper through three decades after the Second World War. In it he made the case that the horses of a nation reflect the national character. An Irish businessman who rides before breakfast to prepare him-self for a day in the office, pulls on a pair of gum boots, rides out into the country-side on his not very highly schooled horse, and skylarks over half a dozen fences. He returns, red in face and blissfully happy, to start the day's work. An Englishman would do much the same but his dress and his horse would be a bit smarter, and he would bear in mind the principles he had learned in Pony Club (walk the last half mile home, etc.). A German, on the other hand, would ride in the indoor school under instruction from his riding master, carrying two dressage whips, one in each hand, to get the hocks well under. And when he has spent an hour achieving perfect obedience and accuracy he is absolutely prepared for his day's work.

We mention this because it illustrates what we believe to be a basic truth, which is that an analysis of horses' performances over the last twenty years or so would show that British, American, Irish, Canadian, Australian, New Zealand and South African showjumpers, as well as eventers, have done better internationally on Thoroughbreds or Irish TB crossbreds than on Continental Warmbloods. They suit these nationalities better because they have more initiative and are less dependent on constant instruction from the rider. They are also, of course, the most wonderful natural athletes. By the same token, the Continental Warmblood suits the Continental rider because of the way they are taught and of atavistic memories of a training regime where complete obedience has been demanded for generations.

The purpose of this book is to show how to set about buying and then making a successful conversion from racehorse to general-purpose animal. Once this has been achieved the horse, depending on his temperament, will be suitable for specialist training in a particular disci-pline – showjumping, eventing, dressage, and so on – or to be used as a pleasure horse for the owner, and one with which they can enjoy riding and any sport at whatever level they fancy.

We hope that our ideas will be useful not only to those who have not done it before, but perhaps to those with experience; for all of us know that we never stop learning about this wonderful athlete who – even though we might study him for over half a century – can still make an awful fool of us on occasions.

If these pages can persuade a few hundred horsemen each year to get hold of a race-horse and turn him into whatever it is that they want for themselves, we shall have reduced the likelihood that those horses will one day be found pulling a metaphorical water cart around the back streets.

GONDOLIER AND RARE MELODY

Lord Howard de Walden very kindly lent us a lovely horse to use for the purpose of this book. Gondolier is an eight-year-old gelding by the Derby winner Slip Anchor out of

The Pedigree of Gondolier

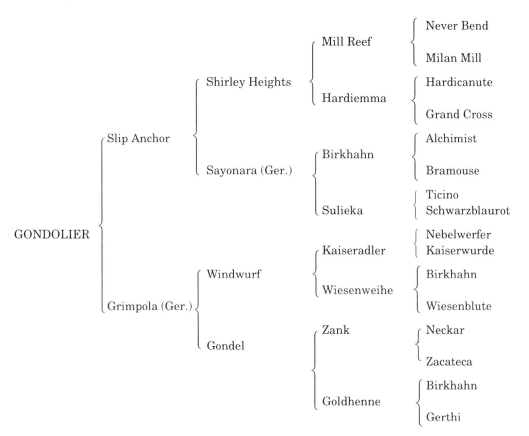

				Never Bend
		Mill Reef		
				Milan Mill
	Shirley Heights			
				Hardicanute
		Hardiemma		
				Grand Cross
Slip Anchor				
				Alchimist
		Birkhahn		
				Bramouse
	Sayonara (Ger.)			
				Ticino
		Sulieka		
				Schwarzblaurot

GONDOLIER

				Nebelwerfer
		Kaiseradler		Kaiserwurde
	Windwurf			
				Birkhahn
		Wiesenweihe		
				Wiesenblute
Grimpola (Ger.)				
				Neckar
		Zank		
				Zacateca
	Gondel			
				Birkhahn
		Goldhenne		
				Gerthi

Grimpola, a German-bred mare. He was a successful racehorse who won three races including the Royal Ascot Stakes and was then second three days later in the Queen Alexandra, both at the Royal meeting in 1992. At that time he was trained by Henry Cecil. In 1994 he won the Doncaster 2000-Rated Stakes for Julie Cecil.

He had his share of woes while he was racing and we shall know more about how sound he is when we come to the end of the book. On initial assessment, he is strong, four-square, beautifully muscled with a great articulation of the hocks and a lovely, long, easy stride. He stands about 16.2hh. He has a good temperament, is perfect in the stable and quick to learn. But he is rather sensitive and loses his nerve easily if you put too much pressure on him. He loves human company and is very affectionate. His stunning action leads us to suspect that if he has the temperament for it he might become an exceptional dressage horse. We shall see.

The second horse featured has been sent to us by Caroline Schweir, a successful eventing and dressage rider who has her stables just down the road from us at

Hargrave. Rare Melody (by Sizzling Melody out of Rare Legend by Rarity) is a four-year-old filly out of training.

I have heard that her sire Sizzling Melody (who was trained by Lord John Fitzgerald to be one of the best sprinters – 5 furlongs – of his generation) is also the sire of some horses with exceptional jumping ability. This is an example of why it is vital to our breeding of successful performance horses that all competition horses are registered on a data base, such as the one run by Wetherbys in the UK. Our breeding of Thoroughbreds for racing in this country is as good as any in the world and the recording of every facet of breeding and racing performance is available to everyone in that industry. If our Thoroughbreds provide us with an unending source of talented performance horses for most disciplines other than racing, then it surely behoves us to establish as much information for those disciplines as we have for the turf. Then, and only then, will breeders be able to assess all the options available to them in the same way that racehorse breeders have done for generations.

Rare Melody hated being trained and never ran. Caroline has made a great purchase. Rare Melody has excellent conformation and, at only four, is strong and four-square and looks every inch a competition horse. I will eat my hat if she doesn't turn into a good jumper. She stands about 16.1½hh. I believe that she got very screwed up in training, and she needs to be handled and ridden with extreme sensitivity, but she is very quick to learn and, like Gondolier, loves people and attention. She seems, at the start of her training here, a very good prospect. She started ten days later than Gondolier.

The reschooling of these two horses comprises five separate stages.

Stage 1   Turn out to relax.
Stage 2   Loose schooling.
Stage 3   Ride away.
Stage 4   Basic schooling.
Stage 5   Where do we go from here?

We shall follow the progress of these two horses from start to finish of this conversion period.

2 Second Career ——————

Before going on to discuss the practicalities of acquiring and reschooling a racehorse, it is worth considering some case histories. These are the stories of some ex-racehorses whose lives have been, so far, happy, useful and successful. They are only a few of very many but the enthusiasm of their owners shows just how wonderful they are and what pleasure they bring. This is what this book is all about. In so many countries, virtually all they have are horses 'off the course' and in those countries standards of performance are often world class. In Britain we cannot afford to waste such an asset. We have racehorses as good as or better than any in the world on which to draw. Among them there are, without any doubt,

Cheval de Guerre, Supreme Champion Hunter, Dublin 1996. Owned by Mr and Mrs G. Wragg and ridden by Mrs Jonah Wragg. (Photo. M. Ansell.)

potential world, European and Olympic gold medalists. There are also many at the other end of the scale that are ready to become ideal riding companions for those who are not concerned with competitions.

THE SHOW RING

One of the most perfect examples of interchangeability is the case of the 1996 Supreme Hunter Champion at Dublin (surely the show world's highest accolade). The champion, Cheval de Guerre, is a five-year-old who was in training until March of that same year, 1996. Muriel Bowen, reporting in *Horse and Hound*, describes him as, 'an attractive five-year-old with presence and a gallop that ate up the arena. Bred by Meadow Stud in Co. Kildare he was sighted in a field by the Wraggs and bought for £10,000 as a three-year-old.'

In March they decided to give him a year off to mature, during which they entered him in the Dublin show to compete, ridden side-saddle by Jonah Wragg, in the Ladies Hunters, which he duly won. This qualified Cheval de Guerre for the most coveted award of all, Dublin's Supreme Hunter Championship. To win this was an extraordinary achievement for a horse so recently out of training and even more so as this proved to be just an interlude before he returns to the racecourse for a career as a 'chaser. A truly romantic story that may yet reach an even more glorious climax.

A further, very interesting, development at Dublin – with much bearing on what we believe is the best way to start reschooling an ex-racehorse – is a class of thirty-four three-year-olds, who had to loose-jump over two fences for a £1,000 first prize, in a class designed to find the show horse that can jump with style (see the photograph on page 84). The *Horse and Hound* commentator wrote, 'It doesn't seem the best way of showing a horse, but big crowds watched and German buyers made copious notes.' It sounds to me as if it fulfilled the two most important objectives of competition at horse shows: to

Philco and David Broome. Look at the athleticism and intelligence of this lovely Thoroughbred, here jumping indoors in Paris. (Photo. Finlay Davidson, supplied by David Broome.)

Jet Run, typical of the world-conquering Thoroughbreds ridden by the US team in the halcyon days of Bertalan de Nemethy. Here Jet Run is winning the gold medal at the Pan American Games in 1979, ridden by Michael Matz. (Photo. Alix Coleman.)

draw the crowds and interest the *cognoscenti*.

SHOWJUMPING

Although it is in the eventing world that these racehorses have come into their own, we cannot overlook the value of the Thoroughbred to showjumping. Those who remember David Broome's grey American ex-racehorse, Philco, will have seen a perfect example. He bought him as a five-year-old in 1973 in the USA. He won £114,000 (a huge sum in those days) and many Grand Prix all over the world, including Calgary in Canada, and represented Great Britain regularly at CSIOs and CSIs (*Concours Saute Internationale*). Of all the many great international horses ridden by David, Philco was amongst the very best and one that he enjoyed as much as any. At that time there were many Thoroughbreds at the top, notably in the United States Equestrian Team. It was the era of Bertalan de Nemethy, probably the world's greatest ever showjumping trainer. He virtually started the sport in

the USA and made his team the best in the world. It was a remarkable achievement.

I spent some years in South Africa where almost all the top showjumpers were 'off the course' and the standard of showjumping was phenomenal. We were treated to another fine example at the Atlanta Olympics in 1996, when Anne Kursinski rode a typical American Thoroughbred (big, bold, scopey) called Echo to help her nation win the team silver medal. It was indeed an echo of the great American clean-bred of the 1970s and 1980s.

DRESSAGE

In dressage, the horse that won the gold medal at the Stockholm Olympic Games (1956) was the Thoroughbred Julie XX ridden by Major Henri St Cyr (Sweden). It was a wonderful combination, and they were victorious in Grand Prix after Grand Prix throughout Europe. St Cyr was a double Olympic Dressage gold medal winner, having also conquered all at Helsinki in 1952 on a horse called Master Rufus. In this same period, Hannelore

19

Major Henri St Cyr, gold medalist at two consecutive Olympic Games. Here he rides his Stockholm 1956 winner, the Thoroughbred Julie XX. (XX is the symbol used on a Continental pedigree to indicate Thoroughbred.)

Weygand, a great German dressage star and Olympic medalist, was at the very top of the tree on another excellent Thoroughbred called Chronist. On the other side of the world, 'M' Kelly rode one of the best dressage horses ever to compete in Australia: MCW, which stood for Melbourne Cup Winner (which he wasn't but he had been bred and trained to be).

HORSE TRIALS

Time and again, all over the world, in the showjumping arena, the show ring, and the dressage manège, the ex-racehorse has proved his extraordinary ability to reach the farmost branches of the Tree of Classical Riding (*see* page 105). But today it is in horse trials that the Thoroughbred, and the ex-racehorse in particular, is pre-eminent. And this is no coincidence: of all breeds, the Thoroughbred is the most versatile, the fastest, the quickest-thinking, the most athletic, and the boldest. These are also the qualities of a good eventer, and it is worth looking at these in more detail.

Versatility

As we have shown, the Thoroughbred can get to the top in most disciplines, and in all the Olympic disciplines. But more than that, he gives you the best ride. Sit on a well-schooled Thoroughbred, or better still, take him out for a good hack, and you will never want anything else. The lightness, self-carriage, comfort and quick response make this horse a nonpareil.

Speed

The further up the tree you go in horse trials, the more significant your speed across country becomes. The slowest racehorse finds this time easier than the fastest Warmblood, and seconds ticking away beyond the time allowed for the course clock up the penalties at an alarming rate. The more advanced the event, the fewer horses are able to complete the course within the time. For this reason, the Thoroughbred is not only less penalized but is also a safer ride. This is because a horse without the easy ground-devouring stride of an animal that has been bred to gallop (and jump) for centuries has to be pushed beyond his natural pace from start to finish. And this is when accidents occur.

We do a lot of interval training with eventers and always explain to riders preparing for three-day-events that in one respect a horse is like a car. Everyone who drives a lot will know that every car has a natural maximum cruising speed. Say, for example, that this is 80 miles per hour. The car will go for ever at that speed and, driving it, you feel that it is well within itself. If you go faster, two things happen: first you get the impression that the increased cruising speed is putting more strain on the car; and, second, you start to use a lot more petrol. So it is with the horse; but the important difference is that the natural cruising speed (at trot as well as canter) increases with fitness. We see on our oval all-weather canter that, as the horse gets fitter, the time gets shorter and shorter – without the riders thinking they are going any faster.

Quick Thinking

Because the Thoroughbred moves more quickly, he has had to learn to think faster. You will see when we come to the chapter on loose schooling that the horses have to think and work out speed and distances to obstacles for themselves. The fact that these horses have a lot of initiative means that when things get into a bit of a muddle on the cross-country course, they are much more likely to be able to find a way out of it than a slower-thinking animal who is more dependent on clear and definite instructions from the rider.

Athleticism

The Thoroughbred is a wonderful natural athlete. He is not descended from the plodding draughthorse but from the highly prized and reared Arabian who was used for the pleasure and sport of eastern potentates while the more humble camel and donkey were used as the beasts of burden. So the frame and muscular structure of the Thoroughbred has been 'designed' for centuries to make the perfect athlete, and that is what he is and what he looks like in action – fit, muscular and gleaming with condition. Of course, his versatility stems in part from his athleticism. He does not find it difficult to carry out any of the activities demanded in

21

any discipline from racing to jumping to dressage.

Boldness

The athletic ability that makes performance easier for Thoroughbreds must also be a contributory factor in making them bold. The occasional tendency for them to be impetuous, though, is a problem that has to be faced. It is certainly not that they have bad or difficult temperaments – far from it. They are, however, both more sensitive and intelligent and so can be more easily spoiled by impatient or crass behaviour. Horses have excellent memories, so what happens to them in their early days is terribly important. Impetuosity can lead them into difficulty, so don't overface them by asking too much too soon. But bring them on right, so that they don't get rattled, and you will have the bravest horse in the whole equine species.

Tina Gifford, Britain's next horse trials superstar, bought General Jock, a marvellous eventer and British team member as everyone knows, at Doncaster sales in 1989 for 4,800 guineas. He was a four-year-old, not well bred in racing terms, and unraced. Racehorse trainers were not interested but Tina's mother, Althea (herself a leading showjumper), liked his style and, with her unerring eye, acquired a horse that has become one of the world's best. Another good horse of Tina's, Harbinger, was first trained as a 'chaser by her famous father, Josh, before he went eventing.

Andrew Nicholson, one of New Zealand's all-conquering event stars, regularly buys at Doncaster's Horses-in-Training-Sale. To encourage readers, Andrew has said:

> A sale is a way to see a lot of horses at one time without the hassle of trailing round the countryside. And 80 per cent of them are there for a good reason: they're too slow for racing. We're not interested in the paper work, we look for something that has presence, catches your eye, and has good limbs, good straight movement and not too much mileage on the clock.

The point that Andrew Nicholson makes about having such a wide choice at a Horses-in-Training Sale is a very valid one. With hundreds to choose from and knowing what you like and what you are looking for, there is every chance of getting a horse to suit your purpose. What is more the cheaper ones will mostly be sold because they are too slow which, for our purpose, doesn't matter in the least.

Some good eventers out of Doncaster include: Andrew Nicholson's Climb the Heights (by Persian Heights out of Charmense by Cut Above), All Honours (Kabour–Tolly's Best by Hittite Glory), and Mark Todd's major winner, Bertie Blunt (Sunyboy–Spanish Harpist by Don Carlos) who raced under the name of Flamenco Lad. Mark Todd also has a promising six-year-old bought out of training at Ascot Sales, Janejolawrieclaire (Scorpio–Burton Princess by Prince Barle). He is renamed Scorch.

Jane Starkey, a regular British Team member in the 1970s and 1980s, has had a number of very successful ex-racehorses. But she had a great triumph in the 1996 Burghley Young Event Horse class. This is a competition where horses are judged on the grounds that they are, or are not, likely to make, international three-day-eventers. The five-year-old Hello Mr Johnstone (Destroyer–Tea Dance by Vitige) did really well and was every inch what the judges were looking for. Jane Starkey had paid a paltry 850 guineas for him at Doncaster as a yearling and sold him on at three for 2,500 guineas in the same sale ring.

Blythe Tait's individual Olympic gold medal winner, Ready Teddy, was in training in New Zealand (when he was called Striking Back). He competed in the Pony Club and in dressage as a five-year-old. He came to the UK by boat at six years old and began his eventing career the following year in March (1995). He upgraded to Intermediate in two months and won his first Intermediate at Goring Heath in May. By October he was Advanced. He had been 11th at his first three-day-event at Blair Castle in August (remember this was just five months after his début as a Novice). In May 1996 he won the 3-star three-day-event at Pratoni del Vivero, Italy and, in July, the Olympic gold medal. This is a perfectly extraordinary and meteoric rise and, as far as I can ascertain, completely without precedent. It speaks volumes for the ex-racehorse but even more for the brilliance of his rider.

Karen Dixon rode to fame as a junior and has not looked back since. She is one of our best and most experienced international and Olympic Team members. Karen has had three good ex-racehorses:

Running Bear by Rubor was bought out of training as a seven-year-old. He was a moderate racehorse trained by Arthur Stephenson. Karen's mother bought him and, eighteen months later in 1982, Karen won the Junior European Championship on him. He completed Badminton,

Karen Straker (now Dixon) on Corriewack on their way to victory in Ireland's premier three-day-event at Punchestown in 1988.

finishing 12th when Karen was just eighteen. In 1983 Bear and Karen were runners-up in the Young Riders European Championships at Burghley and were members of Britain's gold medal team.

Fosseway Surprise by Tin God was bought as an eight-year-old, having been in training with Tim Foster. He was a moderate and unlucky racehorse. Karen's mother, Elaine, watched him at a couple of Novice events, was impressed and bought him for her talented daughter. He became a successful horse at international level and, still fit and well at sixteen (1996), Karen's niece is taking him over for less demanding work.

Corriewack, by Bivouac out of Corrieburn was Karen's third ex-racehorse. His dam, Corrieburn, won the

Foxhunter's Chase at Cheltenham. He was bought from trainer George Fairburn as an unbroken four-year-old, and won the Irish International Three-Day-Event at Punchestown in 1988.

Not all ex-racehorses are destined for fame and glory. They become just wonderful companions with whom to enjoy everyday riding to the full.

THE SCHOOLMASTERS

One of the best second careers is that of the old schoolmaster who has finished racing and is used to teach new generations of jockeys and racing staff at the British Racing School at Newmarket.

There are some pretty good old horses at the Racing School. Here, with the Racing School's senior instructor, Robert Sidebottom, are (from left to right):

Path of Peace *(76 b g) by Warpath out of Turtle Dove. Rider: Christopher Bray. Ran 59 times – 44 Flat, 15 National Hunt (NH): won 15 races (12 Flat, 3 NH); placed 23 (17 Flat, 5 NH). Prize money £70,646. Trainer: C.W. Thornton.*

Shiny Copper *(78 ch g) by Shiny Tenth out of Comprella. Rider: Lee Barber. Ran 52 times – 8 Flat 35 NH (9 in France): won 6, inc. Daily Express Triumph Hurdle (Cheltenham 1982); placed 13. Prize money £23,257. Trainer: Mrs N. Smith.*

Admirals Cup *(78 b g) by Deep Run out of Mirror Buck. Rider: Cheryl Cook. Ran 43 times: won 12 inc. Crockfords Trophy Handicap Chase (Ascot 1984); Plymouth Gin Haldon Gold Cup (Devon & Exeter 1986); placed 14. Prize money £53,870. John Francome's last winner. Trainer: F.T. Winter.*

Migrator *(76 b g) by My Swallow out of Honbichta (Can.). Rider: Craig Cassidy. Ran 65 times – 17 Flat, 48 NH. Prize money £62,977. Won Holsten Diat Pils Hurdle (Sandown 1982); King Well Pattern Hurdle (Wincanton 1983); Welsh Novices Championship Chase (Chepstow 1984). Trainer: Mrs M. Rimmer.*

Another Coral *(83 br g) by Green Shoon out of Myrallette. Rider: Richard Foster. Winner of the Mackeson Gold Cup in 1991 and 9 other chases. Trainer: D. Nicholson.*

Gulfland *(78 ch g) by Gulf Pearl out of Sunland Park. Rider: Hazel Marshall. Ran 69 times: won 11, inc. Siemens Oslo Cup (Ovrevoll) and the amateurs' race at Redcar ridden by HRH The Princess Royal. Placed 24. Prize money £62,992. Trainer: G. Pritchard Gordon.*

3 Finding your Horse

Most of the horses that have finished their racing career are sold at auction. These take place through the year but the majority are in the autumn and early winter. An auction is not the ideal way to buy a horse, but you can – and should – take a vet with you to inspect anything that interests you before the sale. It is important to take a vet who specializes in horses. Small animal or farm livestock vets cannot be expected to be experts on horse conformation. Horse specialists are always to be found where there are Thoroughbred auctions, and in racing, hunting and eventing areas.

The rules governing the purchase of a horse at auction are made clear in the auction catalogue, which should be read

Love at first sight

very carefully before you make a purchase. There may be a vet's certificate lodged in the auctioneer's office, which you should study. Horses can also be returned by the purchaser for certain specified causes and vices but this is only for very limited periods after the sale. These are clearly stated in the catalogue and you must know what they are. So, having bought, you need to be on the ball. Trainers quite often have horses for sale during the season, usually because they are too slow.

FIRST IMPRESSIONS

Whenever you buy a horse the most important thing of all is your first impression. Never try to convince yourself of a horse's assets unless the horse immediately appeals to you. What is more, if you do not like him at first sight don't waste any more of your time or the vendor's. An auction is very stressful for horses, especially if there are lots of people who want to see them out. If you don't want him, don't ask for him to come out of the box.

RACING RECORD

Having decided that you really like him, you must now try to find the down side. If you can, you should check his racing record. For example:

Unraced.
If he is unraced, there must be a reason. It could be that:

- He is unsound. (No good to you.)
- He was ill or injured. (This need not be

a problem if you can be sure that he has recovered fully.)
- He was useless. (Doesn't mean he won't suit your purpose: there are a few horses who just don't enjoy racing.)
- He had a very bad temperament. (No good to you.)
- The owners ran out of funds. (Not a problem to you.)

Ran only once or twice in two years of training.
It could be that:

- He is difficult to keep sound. (No good to you.)
- He is just backward and immature. (Not necessarily a problem to you.)
- He didn't show any sign of talent. (Still might do your job.)

Ran many times over two or more years with or without much success.
If his legs do not show excessive wear (hence the need for a vet to be present):

- He is probably tough and sound.
- He is not easily stressed.
- He has a good temperament.
- If he is a regular winner he is certain to be a trier. (But he is likely to be more expensive unless there is something wrong.)

Ran under both sets of rules (Flat and National Hunt).
The good points mentioned above apply here as well, but there are the following disadvantages:

- He will be older. His competition life will be shorter and resale value less.
- His legs will have suffered more wear and tear.

• He will have been taught to jump fast and flat. We have found that horses that have run over hurdles are often difficult to teach to jump over showjumps cleanly. Especially with combinations, they get faster and flatter so that second and third elements fall far too often.

These disadvantages by no means rule out such a horse but, when making up your mind, they must be taken into account. If, for example, you buy a seven-year-old, he will be nine or even ten before he is in serious eventing. At this age he will be more difficult to sell than if he was two years younger. This may not matter to you in the least.

As we have seen so often, even at the highest level, an eventer that is a bad showjumper can be the cause of dreadful disappointment. For both showjumping and horse trials you need a horse that naturally jumps clear rounds. You can only do so much by good schooling: your horse must have a good technique of his own and not want to hit fences.

Do not give up on a horse just because he was no good as a racehorse. We have known many such horses that just didn't like racing and have gone on to be successful in other fields.

SOUNDNESS

However beautiful, never buy a horse that has a question mark about his soundness. This is why, unless you are a knowledge-able dealer yourself, you need to have a vet's advice. If a horse at auction does not have a vet's certificate you should look at him askance. Even if he does, you should still look at him very carefully. It is very much safer to buy privately when your vet

can do a proper examination and evaluation. Nevertheless thousands of lovely horses are sold at low prices at Thoroughbred auctions and give years of pleasure to their purchasers.

If you do buy a horse at auction you should have a wind test done by your vet the very next day. If he is not right he will be returnable, provided the auctioneer has not declared that 'he has been heard to make a noise', or words to that effect, and that it is not mentioned in the catalogue.

FEET

'No foot, no horse' is a well-worn truism. Good-shaped, sound feet are an absolute *sine qua non* so don't try to kid yourself that your farrier can put right what nature or incompetence have ruined. Of course he can rectify bad shoeing, but only if no permanent damage has been caused. Badly balanced feet, a box foot, insufficient hoof wall to nail a shoe on, contracted heels, dropped soles, or just badly shaped feet are all no-nos. Here is yet another reason why you must have a vet to help you unless you really understand all this.

This is such an important subject that we have asked Stephen Gowing, who is our excellent farrier, to write a piece about what to look for and what to avoid. This is included as Appendix 1.

VICES

Box-walking, weaving, wind-sucking, crib-biting are all reasons why a horse can usually be returned. These vices can sometimes be cured, or you may like a horse so much that you are prepared to put up with it. But there are real problems ahead if you are. For a start they are infectious, insofar as one horse copies another. Thus you may, as we found in a stable recently, end up with several horses in one yard all wind-sucking. This can result in colic, flatulence and inability to get into good condition and fit for serious work.

The vices are signs, especially in the case of box-walking or weaving, of a temperament that is easily stressed. A horse with an equable, easy-going nature is more likely to be a source of pleasure and happiness than one that is too highly strung. But the vices may be no more than signs of boredom and this is easier to put right by making the horse's life more entertaining.

TEMPERAMENT

Temperament is a major factor in your enjoyment of your horse. By and large, those that love the company of people and have come to realize that, as Xenophon puts it, 'solitude means hunger and thirst and teasing horseflies, while food, drink and relief from pain come from man,' are the ones that give back most in return. If you are buying a horse for yourself you want one that will give you his absolute trust so that he knows that if you say 'Do this,' 'Go there,' or 'Jump that,' he will because he believes it is safe.

It is not difficult to assess whether a horse has a good temperament:

It is not difficult to assess whether a horse has a good temperament.

- He is undisturbed when people go in and out of his stable.
- He tends to turn towards you and not away.
- He stretches his muzzle towards you with his ears forward and a calm look in his eye.
- When someone goes to put a headcollar or bridle on him he accepts it freely, even eagerly.
- He leads willingly and without hesitation in and out of his stable.
- He stands quietly and proudly while people examine him.
- He leads up at walk and trot steadily and calmly.

All the above are indications (not complete but certainly meaningful) that he is the sort of horse to make a good companion. This impression is enhanced if you can watch him saddled for riding:

- Does he make you think that he is pleased that he is going to be ridden?
- Does he accept the saddle and being girthed up?
- Does he stand still while the rider gets on?
- Does he walk forward freely and quietly when he moves off?
- Does he behave admirably when ridden round the pre-sale ring?
- Will he stand quietly and with an easy rein while his rider stops to talk to someone?
- Does he walk calmly and happily round the sale ring, full of trust and confidence?

Failing some of these stringent tests is not a reason for not buying him if you have taken a liking to him; but each test passed can add to your high opinion. On the other hand, if at any stage he shows panic or stubborness or serious unco-operation, it is probably better to leave him to a professional and look again for yourself.

CONFORMATION

Conformation is about design, and design is all about function. A well-designed teapot is not just pretty: it pours tea without spilling or dribbling, it doesn't scald your hand when holding the handle, and it does not balance so precariously that it is easily knocked over. A teapot that is only a thing of great beauty but does not fulfil these criteria ends up in a glass-fronted cupboard while the functional one does sterling duty over a long period of time.

So it is with the horse. We say 'What a lovely horse' because experience has taught us that a horse designed like that is more likely to perform in the way we want. We never say this about an animal with a pretty head and crooked limbs. Having said that, Claudius Crozet was trained by Geoff Huffer to win ten races on the flat and over hurdles over a period of six years. He had the worst front legs I ever saw and was blind in one eye from a foal, having lost it in an accident. He went on until he was eighteen as Victoria's hack, eventually being put down when a long-quiescent cancer erupted. He was a super ride and loved by everybody. My wife hunted him, and one day a splendid huntswoman rather haughtily asked her why she hunted in blinkers! It was his eyepatch that he always wore in public to disguise his unsightly scar, to stop the eye socket from watering, and to prevent flies from getting into it.

Nevertheless, it makes sense that a horse

A well-balanced horse of near-perfect conformation. He can be divided into four equal parts: poll to breast; breast to back of withers; withers to point of hip; hip to back of quarters.
   This statue used to stand outside the late Lord Derby's Woodland Stud, Newmarket. It was bequeathed in his will to the Jockey Club, who moved it to it's present site in the Courtyard outside the Jockey Club Rooms in the High Street, where it gives much pleasure to visitors and the townsfolk of racing's headquarters.

whose design – conformation – indicates that he is capable will be more likely to perform satisfactorily than one who starts off with a conformational disadvantage.

Balance

The first thing to look for is balance. By this we mean that a horse should be divided into four equal parts. If one of these parts is either too long or too short the horse is considered to be not well balanced. Horses with short necks or not much length of rein never give you the confidence that they will put you back in the saddle in a crisis. And such an outline is not pleasing to a dressage judge.

Balance can be seen in the lovely statue of the immortal Hyperion, bred in 1930 by the 17th Earl of Derby. A chestnut son of Gainsborough (who was himself a triple crown winner), Hyperion was only 15.1½hh. when he won the Derby in record time. To make up for his small stature he had near-perfect conformation, and, as

31

Peter Willett said of him in *The Classic Racehorse*, 'a sweeping action at the gallop which expressed the graceful movements of the Thoroughbred in their most exquisitely developed form.' He went on to become one of the most influential sires, worldwide, of the twentieth century, passing on not only his great brilliance and soundness but also his ideal temperament. I myself had a nice grandson of his whom I reschooled as a polo pony after he finished racing, and who went on to play for South Africa.

LIMBS

The line-drawings show how a horse should stand if his conformation is correct, as well as faults to note and, in some cases, avoid altogether when buying. Again, if you are not an expert, look for these faults but consult your vet about how serious they are and whether they are bad enough to make it unwise to risk your money.

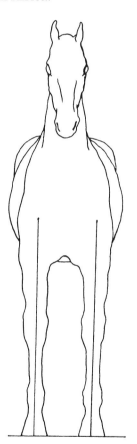

Correct stance.

Front view.

The front leg viewed from the side.

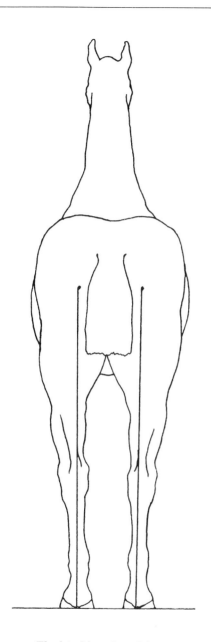

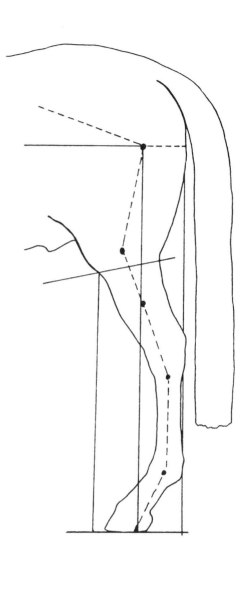

The hind leg viewed from behind.

The hind leg viewed from the side.

Weakness and defects of the front legs.

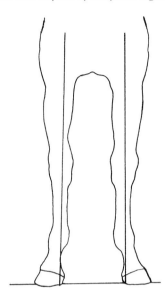

Splay-footed; twisted at the fetlock. Such a horse would never stay sound.

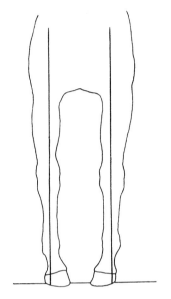

Pigeon-toed. A less serious fault, but undesirable nonetheless.

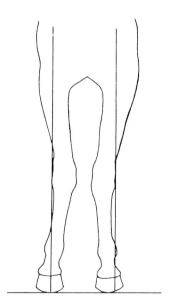

Knock-kneed. This fault sets up great strains in the legs.

Over at the knee. Unsightly but less serious.

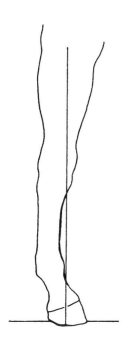

Back at the knee (or calf-kneed). This is a serious fault.

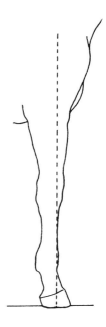

A straight pastern, which means that it is not effective as a shock absorber. This fault causes strain on the limbs and makes for an uncomfortable ride.

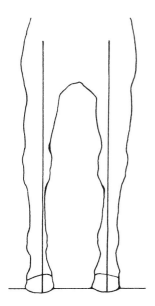

Bow-kneed. This puts strain on the limbs.

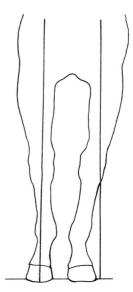

Too close at the ground. A horse with this fault is unlikely to stay sound.

Weaknesses and defects of the hind leg.

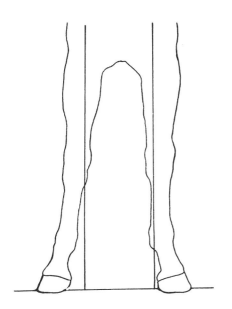

Too wide at the ground; knees turned out. The leg is twisted, which means that the horse is unlikely to stay sound.

Sickle-hocked. This is a weakness likely to lead to curbs. However, it is not too important and actually helps to produce forward movement.

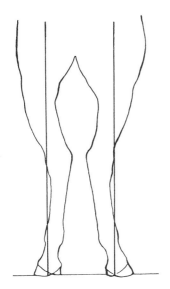

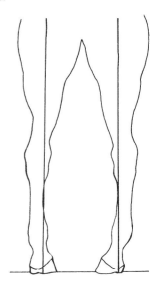

Cow-hocked: a weakness.

Bandy-legged. As well as being unsightly, this fault produces strain on the fetlock joints.

It is obvious that these examples are not how an engineer would design the legs to withstand the enormous strain of galloping, jumping or prolonged periods of work. The faults can occur in greater or lesser degree, and how critical they are is best decided by a vet. When in doubt it is sensible not to take a risk. Remember that it costs just as much to keep a bad horse as it does a good one.

We are particularly averse to horses that are thick through the throat. They cannot flex properly at the poll, which means that they hold their heads always forward of the vertical. They are incapable of achieving any degree of collection, can't soften through their neck and back, find it very difficult to get off their forehand and, therefore, can never give you a good ride. You should easily be able to put your clenched fist between the jaw bones. Between the cheekbone and the neck there should be a deep, wide valley that lets the horse drop his nose so that the front line of the head is vertical to the ground.

So that nothing is overlooked, we have an *aide-mémoire* to help you to assess a horse before deciding whether to buy him or not. It is perfectly straightforward in that it lists the conformational points you need to examine:

This filly is thick through her throat. There is no deep valley behind her cheekbone. The result is that she finds it difficult to flex at the poll, and her head is always stuck forward.

Gondolier is lovely in this respect. As a result he has perfect head carriage, which means that he is soft through his back and neck, and into your hands.

CONFORMATION: Assessment of horse
before purchase.

Head:
Neck:
Shoulders:
Back:
Quarters:
Near Foreleg:
Off Foreleg:
Near Hind Leg:
Off Hind Leg:
Feet:

Heart Room:
Width:
Depth of Girth:
Length:
Depth:

Hip to Tail:
Hip to Stifle:
Hip Width:

Knees:
Hocks:
Fetlocks:
Pasterns:
Cannon Bones:
Fore Arm:

Temperament:
General Condition:
Coat:
Blemishes:

Other Remarks:

ACTION

After spending more than half a century with horses, we have come to the conclusion that there are only two common denominators that apply to all good horses:

1. A pronounced articulation of the hock joint at all paces.

If a horse moves his hind leg all in one piece without flexing his hocks we advise you leave him well alone. This is not to say that a horse that has good articulation is necessarily good, but it is certain that all good horses have this attribute. It is true of all performance horses, whether they are racehorses, eventers, jumpers, driving horses, dressage or whatever, and I think that – as with the thickness through the throat – you can never get a really good ride from a horse that doesn't use his hocks properly.

It is always said that the engine is at the back of a horse and the part of the engine that drives him forward is the hocks. It is obvious, really, that if he flexes his hocks, lifting his feet high, and then puts them down well underneath him, he will propel himself forwards – and upwards if he is jumping – much more effectively than if he does not.

2. Of equal importance to the first is freedom of the shoulder.

Unless a horse has a lovely loose swing of the shoulder and front leg he will never gallop and go forward with long, easy, ground-devouring strides that exhaust neither horse nor rider. The illustration on page 32, shows the skeleton of the front leg. It is really important that the shoulder blade is angled well backward (more so, perhaps, than shown in the drawing) so that the stride is lengthened. Similarly a shoulder that is more vertical, which is often coupled with a straight pastern, will give a short, jarring, uncomfortable stride. The reason is obvious. The two shock-absorbing joints of the shoulder and the fetlock are going to be much more inefficient, and any vehicle with poor shock-absorbers is bound to be uncomfortable.

The front legs must be on the outside of the chest so that all the bones of these limbs can swing straight and freely forwards and backwards.

Given these attributes you will get a lovely free-going, easy swinging action and that is what you want. You are able to judge how good this is by watching where the feet fall at walk and trot. What we are about to describe is essential and if a horse doesn't do it, don't go for him. It must happen without any force whatever and when your horse is just walking along (or trotting) completely relaxed.

The walk is a four-time movement in which the feet touch the ground as shown in the diagram. That is, left hind, left front, right hind, right front. The four-time beat must be exactly even. When coming through at the walk the hind foot (1) must step well beyond the imprint just left by the front foot (2). By well over I mean about 46cm (18 in).

The trot is a two-time movement in which the feet touch the ground as shown in the next diagram. He dances from one diagonal to the other and at this pace the hind foot must fall exactly into the imprint of the front foot on the same side. This is called 'tracking up', and it is essential that it happens.

I will go as far as to say that if the foot-fall is not as described here you would be

The order in which the feet touch the ground at walk.
1 2 3 4

The order in which the feet touch the ground at trot.
1 2

better to leave that horse and look for another if you are hoping to compete successfully in any discipline.

Straightness of action is important. Plaiting, where the swing of the leg is an inward curve is a serious fault. Not only is the horse likely to do himself an injury when one leg hits another, but he is also going to put his feet down with the toes pointing out, putting strain on the whole leg. Dishing, if not too pronounced, is usually not serious and many good horses even excellent racehorses – dish to a greater or lesser extent. But the ideal is a straight, free action with a well-defined and determined foot-fall.

With all the hard ground of a dry summer you do not want a horse that pounds into the ground. I love to see a horse that canters or lands over a fence with such a light foot-fall that, as they say, you couldn't hear it if you put a stethoscope on it.

A final point about action. When you look at a horse walking away from you,

This gorgeous two-year-old colt by Nashwan out of Chief Celebrity dishes (as can be seen in this photograph). I can forgive him anything because he is so beautiful, a stunning mover and marvellous ride. His jockey, Bizzie Budden, was sorry when he left for Japan.

you should see a noticeable swing of the quarters as each hind leg moves forward. It is a real indication of a classy horse and is accompanied by a rhythmical, pronounced and wave-like swing of the tail.

SEX

The horse you have set your heart on may be a colt. Don't be put off by this but, if you buy him, do have him gelded. If you are a serious breeder, of course, you may want to keep him entire with the plan of using him as a stallion later on. But normal competitive riders do not want stallions: it greatly complicates life and geldings are easier, calmer and more straightforward in every way. When you do have him gelded, take the advice of your vet. Hope that he will give him a five-day course of antibiotics. Experience has taught us that you should carry on with whatever exercise he was taking, the very next day. If he can be taken out again in the afternoon, so much the better. By doing this you will decrease the risk of excessive inflammation around the incision and consequent complications. Keep the incision clean by hosing it gently with cold water as often as you can manage. The bed must be immaculate and droppings removed straight away. Bed him on straw or paper, not on shavings which get into the scar.

A noticeable swing of the quarters.

Mares, although some people think they don't want them, are wonderful. When you get a good one she will jump off the end of the earth for you. I have had several brilliant mares who gave me the most perfect rides. And history shows that many of the best competition horses have been female.

KEEPING PERSPECTIVE

Throughout this chapter we have been issuing dire warnings about what to avoid to such an extent that you may feel that you will never find a horse that meets these stringent standards. If you look at successful horses it will be obvious that the perfect horse is almost non-existent. All faults occur to a greater or lesser degree, and you (and your adviser) must make your mind up and decide what you can overlook and what is bad enough to rule a horse out. Don't forget that the first impressions are often the best so that if you really fall for a horse at once he is likely to be the right one for you. I remember the late Brigadier Lyndon Bolton, who had a great eye for a good horse, saying that insecure judges can be taken to a stable, the door opened to reveal a magnificent horse, and all that they see is a curb.

4 Early Management

TURNING OUT

When you have selected and bought your ex-racehorse the first thing to do is to turn him out for a good break. His racing career will probably have taken quite a lot out of this young horse and he needs a complete change of environment and activity.

Don't, of course, take him straight out of racing and chuck him out into a field and forget about him. He must be let down gradually over a period of a week or two. Everything depends on his temperament and the time of the year. Ideally you want to be able to turn him out while there is still some goodness in the grass. But you have to make the transition from hard food to grass quite carefully. It is a big change of diet, especially if he has been stabled without a break for a year or two. I think most racehorse owners and trainers nowadays like to give their horses a rest between seasons in any case and lots of them go back to their studs or their owners' private stables to get away from the hurly-burly of a racing yard, and if this has been the case with your horse then so much the better.

Whatever your plan, the first thing to do is to give your horse a thorough health check-up – the equivalent to a car's service. It is important to make sure he is in good physical shape when you take him out and

to continue to apply good management practices.

WORMING

You probably have your own routine, but for the first three months we recommend worming once a month. Use three different drugs to make sure that as wide a spectrum as possible has been covered.

Normal worming preparations should be sufficient but in the rare case that you get a horse with a bad infestation your vet will produce something even more effective.

After the first three months you can go to one dose every six weeks. But revert to monthly when your horse is at grass.

Give your horse a thorough service.

THE MOUTH

By and large it is a complete misconception that racehorses have ruined mouths. A horse that has been in National Hunt racing may have become used to pulling your arms out, but he will probably be older than the horse you are looking for and, in any case, any mouth can be improved out of recognition if the teeth are right and the reschooling is well done. A three- or four-year-old flat racehorse should present little or no problem. By the time you have finished the loose-schooling regime it will have been several months since the horse had a bit in his mouth and any bruising or discomfort will have long gone.

This loose-schooling period, as you can see from the photographs, will see the horse doing all the things that you think you do through your hands and reins. I am talking about steering, changes of direction, collection, extension, stretching forward and downward, and so on. Watching it all happen without a bit, reins or hands will help you to become much more sensitive when you start using those aids again. I have never found a problem in making a good educated mouth for a young horse off the racecourse.

Teeth

No amount of food and worm dosing will get your horse looking and feeling right if

44

his teeth need attention.

If he has wolf teeth, now is the time to have them out. It is a routine with us. They generally cause great discomfort, head-shaking, refusal to accept the bit and inattention to the job in hand and we advise you to have them out in every case.

If you don't know how to feel your horse's teeth, get your vet to do it. Sharp outside edges to the molars can cut and lacerate the inside of the cheek, making the mouth terribly sore as well as preventing your horse from grinding his food properly. The result is undigested food that leaves the horse in much the same form as it was when it was ingested at the other end, having done absolutely no good to anyone but your feed merchant in between.

If you buy a three-year-old, make sure that the caps on his molars (which were his milk teeth) have come out. Sometimes they get stuck and become embedded in his gums. Obviously this is very painful and irritating and makes grinding food impossible. You can often tell that this has happened by the awful smelly breath that results when food becomes trapped beneath these caps. You can sometimes remove them by hand if you know how, or with a small pair of pincers.

The incisor milk teeth are also uncomfortable while they are being replaced by the permanent teeth. Again it is a good practice to help them on their way when they are about to fall out.

PHYSIOTHERAPY

If you use the services of an equine therapist this is the time to have your new acquisition checked over and treated if necessary. This should be done with the agreement of your vet. Most up-to-date vets nowadays agree that this treatment by a qualified practitioner is an essential aspect of looking after an equine athlete. We all know that top human athletes don't move without their physiotherapist in attendance. And when you think about it, they don't have somebody sitting on the weakest part of their back while they are racing, jumping or playing football! There are so many misconceptions about equine physiotherapy that we have asked our brilliant therapist Sarah Culverwell to clear up some of these. Her remarks are contained in Appendix II.

APPETITE

It is important to make sure that your horse has a good appetite. He won't have if worms, teeth or a backache are making him feel miserable. But if those are all sorted out and he is still a shy feeder then you must really go to work and tempt him to enjoy and look forward to his meal times. Horses can get 'over-proteined' when kept on high-protein regimes for long periods. Their system rebels and they stop eating altogether; it is nature taking avoiding action. A nice grassy paddock will do the trick – total change of diet and low protein. It will give the over-burdened system a rest. Linseed, too, is a slow poison if it is fed continuously. There is always a reason for loss of appetite and, when you have found it, it is comparatively simple to put things right.

Some people think that if you make the feed too delicious in order to get a horse to eat, he will go off his food again when he returns to a more standard diet. This is not the case. We have said before that horses are creatures of habit: once they get the habit of eating they will continue to do so. Everyone knows how difficult it is to go on a diet when your stomach has become used to gargantuan Christmas meals. It is just the same with horses. Once their insides have got used to telling them that they are hungry they will eat up properly.

There are many additions you can use to liven up a diet and there are many delicious prepared feeds nowadays that are full of taste and variety. Persevere until you have found the key to unlock the appetite, and use things like apples, carrots, molasses and freshly cut grass to tempt the taste buds.

Never leave stale food in the manger, and keep the manger clean. Feed little and often (at least three times a day). Get your horse into the habit of cleaning up. Hay is terribly important. It must be clean and virtually dust-free. A shy feeder is never going to finish up his hay if it smells more like tobacco. It must have what is called 'a good nose' to it. I get furious if I find hay thrown out onto the muck heap because it means it was tainted by rats, mice, cats, dogs, chickens! If you get top-quality hay look after it. A fussy feeder won't go near it if the world and his wife have walked over it with dirty feet. He may also be put off if too much is given. Much better to give him what he will clear up; so 'little and often' is the watchword.

BLOOD

Most horses off the racecourse will be pretty healthy, but if you are not happy, get your vet to take a blood sample to test. If there are deficiencies he will prescribe treatment that will save you much worry

and will help you get your horse into the condition you want without delay.

COAT

The condition of your horse's coat is an indication of how well he is. It must not only glisten, it must feel lovely to your hand. Smooth and silky, you should be able to take a fistful of loose skin on the neck or shoulder which must return quickly to its normal state when you let go.

All these things, though, come right not just when there is a low worm count, the teeth are in perfect trim, there are no problems for the physiotherapist, and the blood is correct: they come from work. It is the right sort of work that makes the horse look great with a magnificent sleek coat covering the physique of an equine athlete.

SHOES

Before turning your horse out, his feet must be prepared. The ideal is to put him out without shoes, but you can't do this if his feet are brittle and the ground is hard. In all you have three options:

Shoes Off

This is the best option if conditions are right. If you choose this, the feet must be trimmed quite seriously but, of course, without making him lame. Make sure your farrier gets the best balance and hoof/pastern axis possible (*see* Appendix I) as these next few weeks give you the ideal opportunity to restore any man-induced harm to his feet. While he is out the feet

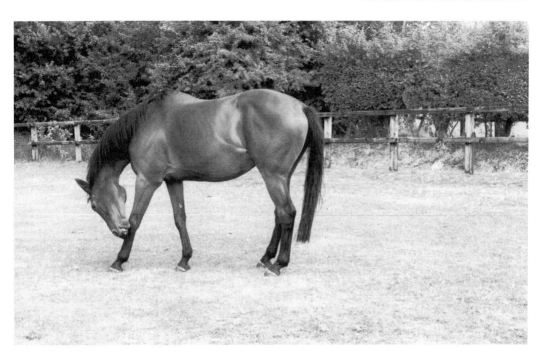

Gondolier happily turned out at Lord Howard de Walden's Plantation Stud after ending his racing career. He is pretending he doesn't want to be caught . . .

. . . by anyone other than the stud groom Patrick Lennon.

must be regularly trimmed to make absolutely sure that they don't get into a state where they are likely to break or crack. If there is the slightest danger of this he must be either shod in front or, if necessary, shod all round.

Shod in front

While he is not working it is truly important that your farrier takes great care with balance and hoof/pastern axis as described above. If it becomes necessary to shoe in front, the hind feet must not be neglected: they must be kept trimmed and you must be careful to check regularly that they are not also becoming brittle.

Shod all round

This is the least satisfactory option and should only be chosen if the feet are very brittle.

THE PADDOCK

A secure, sheltered paddock, with cover from rain, wind and sun, and a permanent water supply is required. If all this is available there is no need to bring him in at night. However, if all you have is an open paddock, then he should be turned out through the day and stabled at night. This is not so good, as we want him to be switched right off.

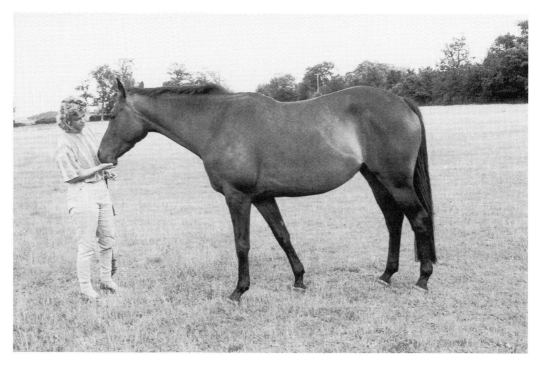

Caroline Schweir with Rare Melody at the end of her rest period on the farm of David and Cherry Barclay.

How long you leave him out depends on your timetable and the fact that you will probably want to have the job done before winter begins. A horse doesn't have a calendar and I am sure can't tell the difference between, say, three months or four. However I think the minimum time at complete rest should be six weeks.

If the grass is good and succulent there is probably no need to supplement at all. However, if it is poor and drought-stricken you will have to feed as well because at the end of the rest period you want a plump, contented animal to start the next phase – loose schooling. In winter, horses use a lot of feed just keeping warm, so in inclement weather horses that are turned out must be fed like fighting cocks. We have had many, many Thoroughbreds turned out all winter and they always come in looking brilliant. But it costs. When you get him in, check all the points of the physical check-up that we have already described and you are ready for action.

5 In the Loose School

For the next month or so, Gondolier and Rare Melody are going to be working in the loose school. The period of turn out should have relaxed them and helped them put the pressures of life in a racing yard behind them. Working in the loose school, which will be absolutely new to them, will get them going again in as stress-free a way as possible. In no time at all they find it fun: they really have to think for themselves and you can truly see how much they enjoy the learning process.

When you are introducing your horse to something new, like this, there are two golden rules that must always be borne in mind:

1.   Never go on too long.
2.   Always finish when your horse has done something really well.

We work in the loose school with no tack whatsoever except a headcollar (which you can also take off if you like, once you are sure that you can catch your horse again without a problem.) We always use leather

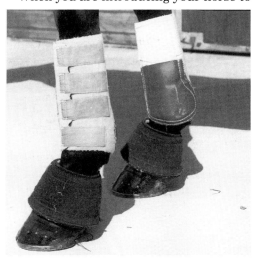

Front and back boots and overreach boots are essential when loose schooling.

They are doubly important when training young horses who are inexperienced in loose schooling.

If he gets excited stay cool.

headcollars. Nylon will burn your hand if he pulls away from you, and it will not break if it becomes caught in something.

Your horse must have boots on in front and behind as well as over-reach boots, because when he is loose and fooling about he may easily hit himself.

THE SCHOOL

An indoor school makes an ideal loose school. In order to get good pictures, however, we needed more light and so we set one up outside using the invaluable mesh pens that we use for lungeing and turning out. The size is 25×16m (27 × 17.5) yards with round ends. The gate should be

at the end furthest from the route to the school. This is to overcome any tendency to stop at the entrance. It has to be at the end of the school because all your exercises and jumps are on the long side and you don't want them thinking about the exit while they are working over them.

Using a pen this size you need two people. As always we insist that those who are working the horse wear hard hats and good footwear so that they don't slip (*see* diagram on p.60).

THE APPROACH

During the period of loose schooling you must never be in a hurry. Assume that your horse has had a stressful life so far and is likely to be uptight as he starts something completely new. If he gets excited and doesn't pay any attention to you, stay cool.

If you keep calm, it is certain that within a week to ten days he will be happily laid back, relaxed and at ease with his work.

When Rare Melody came, she would not walk through the door into her stable. We knew she had a problem loading into the starting stalls when she was in training. So no one got excited about it or pushed her, and within twenty-four hours this little problem was a thing of the past. Similarly Caroline told us that the mare was very whip-shy – and so she was – but it was only a week before we were able to touch her with it and run it across her

back and down over her quarters without her showing any sign of anxiety.

Everything possible must be done to win the horse's trust and confidence, hence the need to avoid making an 'issue' out of anything and to keep calm at all times. A horse that is encouraged to feel relaxed and confident will be far more willing to co-operate than one that is made to feel anxious.

The Environment

At this stage what goes on inside the stable will be of great help in getting the results we want outside. Stable management in the racing industry is

Emma Haigh, our yard manager, runs the whip across the back of Rare Melody, who really couldn't care less.

generally of a very high standard and a great proportion of stable staff care much for the well being of their charges. The odds are, therefore, that your ex-racehorse will be well used to an affectionate environment in which he is given the best of everything. Obviously there are exceptions in horses that find it hard to settle down to the demands of a racing regime.

The new environment must be such that the new horse is made to feel safe and cared for. The more time, within reason, that the new owner or his groom (or both) can spend with him the more at ease he is going to be. In such a frame of mind it is going to be simpler to achieve what we are now setting out to do.

This does not mean that everyone who passes by should touch the horses. We hate this and so, we think, do they. We don't believe in being anthropromorphic, but how would you like it if everyone who walked past you tried to touch your face? Ugh! They are persons; let them have their dignity.

OBJECTIVES

Our objectives in loose schooling are that the horse will be able to:

• Go equally well in both directions.
• Trot over poles on the ground without hurrying the pace or hitting the poles.
• Jump small fences and gymnastic exercises calmly, in good style, and boldly, without hitting the obstacles.

How do we do that?

The first thing to say is that we can't put a timetable on our progress. Each horse

tells us when he is ready to go on to the next stage. It is important to 'hasten slowly', otherwise you will get your horse rattled, which is a step backward and not hastening at all! For a horse whose whole life has been concerned with wide open spaces and speed it is a very big change to be led into an enclosed area and have to pick your way over and across what may seem a confusing mass of poles. As the horse finds it easier and easier and becomes calmer and calmer, you will know exactly when the time comes to ask a little more.

The Lessons

What we are trying to teach them during this period is:

• To obey the voice and willingly do what is wanted.
• To relax.
• To use the right muscles and go in a good shape.
• To learn to look where they are going and put their feet in the right place.
• To develop their brain power so that they can assess a situation and come up with the right answer.
• To learn that this is achieved by following their trainer's wishes and that resistance makes it more difficult. And thus,
• To love the teamwork with their trainers and try to do the right thing, both because it is easier and because they appreciate the plaudits and affection that this brings (not to mention the mints).

At all stages they must find it easy and fun.

BODY LANGUAGE

Before going on to demonstrate precisely what should be done in the first few days of loose schooling, it is worth pausing to look more closely at the means by which we will achieve our initial aims.

By nature horses flee from that which they don't know or understand. It comes from being a herd animal. We have all seen films of herds of animals in flight from danger. But we have also seen how inquisitive they are, how they long to find out about something that might be a danger but might not, and how they take a step towards it – every sense of sight, sound and smell straining to find out – while at the same time they are poised for instant flight.

We have seen how animals seek a place of safety: the cub, calf or foal, the security of its mother; all animals, their home, be it hole, earth, lair or stable; the herd animal, the security of anonymity within the group.

We have observed two interesting patterns of instinctive behaviour, one in older horses, the other in very young ones. If you are riding out in company on an older horse and, for some reason, you have a fall and something frightens him so that he runs off, he will usually go home and you will find him waiting smugly for you in his stable when you get back. If you are out with string of young horses and one of them gets loose he will dash off for a short distance, stop, wonder what to do next until the herd instinct takes over and he comes back to the others. The first demonstrates the need to return to his place of safety, the second to anonymity within the herd.

Nevertheless if real panic strikes – and sometimes we have seen this when an improperly fitted saddle slips round under the horse's belly – he will just run and run in blind fear until he can run no longer. A truly horrible sight and unforgivable.

These are the instincts built into our horses. We must understand and use these instincts throughout our training so that we come to represent to them a haven that is steadfast, trustworthy and reliable. We must mean to the horse safety and protection and ease of mind.

Our body language – the way we move and present ourselves to the horse – is the primary means by which we convey a sense of these things to him. And it is through our body language that the horse will come to understand what is expected of him. Communication takes place, and thus our movements and his – each responding to the other – can be compared to a dance in which we are the leader and the horse the follower. We give the signal, the horse concurs. We move behind his movement to signal 'Go on a bit', and we step towards him to say 'Go out' (on the lunge or in the loose school). In doing this we are utilizing our understanding of his instinct for flight to teach him 'Go away'. Once he associates these movements of ours with what he is supposed to do, the flight is forgotten but the signal remains.

Thus, too, when we want him to slow down we move a little ahead of his movement (to prevent him from coming off the track or turning in), and then lower our voice and our whip and move away from him (the danger no longer threatens) so that he can relax knowing that we provide the haven he might have needed.

You will observe that when we get him to stop, using our voice as well as our body

Polo-mint time. A haven.

movement, his automatic response is to turn and come to us. And he must be taught that this is OK – but only when we call him – and that when he comes to us he can put his head under our arm to hide from the mock danger that he no longer fears and be rewarded with stroking and gifts and affection and comfort. For he is the child who, not in the least frightened, comes back to its mother every now and then just for a spot of reassurance.

In our dance, our body language is the direction of influence by which we lead our partner through all the movements that make the partnership so enjoyable.

FIRST DAYS

We lead our pupil to the school in a Chifney. He is then taken two or three times in each direction around the school to make him realize that there is nothing to worry about. When he is let go, however, he will undoubtedly find all sorts of things to shy at; and there will probably be one place that he decides is particularly alarming and at which, on every circuit, he will refuse point blank to stay out beside the wall. You see, he doesn't know what you want and he certainly hasn't discovered that what you want is actually the easiest thing for him to do. He hasn't got

55

First, Kate Hodgkins leads Gondolier around the manège so that he knows both what it is like and that he is meant to keep close to the outside wall.

to know you yet either – you still have to gain his trust. He is showing that he does not trust you yet.

Once he has been led around and has settled down, turn him into the school off the track and take off the Chifney by undoing the cheekpiece and slipping the bit out of his mouth while you keep hold of the headcollar.

We once knew someone whose jaw was broken by a kick when he went to turn a horse out. Always turn him towards you so that he can't kick as he moves away. Hence also the importance of wearing a hard hat. A kick as you let him go is just as likely to be high spirits as a deliberate or malicious act, but the effect is exactly the same.

You and your partner now have the task of keeping the horse out beside the fence.

You do this by using the position of your body, the lunge whip and your voice.

Your first problem is likely to be that as soon as you release him into the manège he will set off at a fast, undisciplined pace which will probably be something like a very inelegant running trot interspersed with strides of canter. Now is the time to do *nothing*. Do not attempt to stop him; just let him get it out of his system while you stand and watch, but keep your eyes and mind focused on him all the time. Before long, he will realize that all this dashing about is getting him nowhere and he will start to slow down. Only at this stage will you be able to gain his attention and start to teach him, and it is the point at which it is crucial that you take charge. You do this by not allowing him to stop, which is precisely what he will want to do

If he starts dashing round, do nothing except to prevent him turning round or stopping. He will soon settle down.

now that he has discovered that there is nothing for him to gain by racing around. This is very important. The cardinal sin is to let him turn round or stop without being asked. You have waited while he did what he wanted to do, so now you must in effect say to him, 'No, don't stop. Get to work now and carry on round the school – but at a pace dictated by me.'

Of course, you don't say it in so many words. You have to decide on a vocabulary that you will consistently use to teach him to understand what you want from him. We use:

Walk
Walk on
Trot
Canter
Slowly
Stand
Stand still
Change
Come here

It is not so much the actual words, but rather the tone of voice, that enables your horse to understand what you want. You must therefore have a different tone for each command. But always use the same word and the same tone and you will find that in about a week he will be more or less obedient to the voice. Don't put a question mark after your command. It must not be 'Walk on?' but 'Walk on!'.

So, having dashed around the arena until he realizes he has had enough, your horse, like Gondolier, decides to stop. But you – keeping just behind his movement (but not so far behind that he can turn in

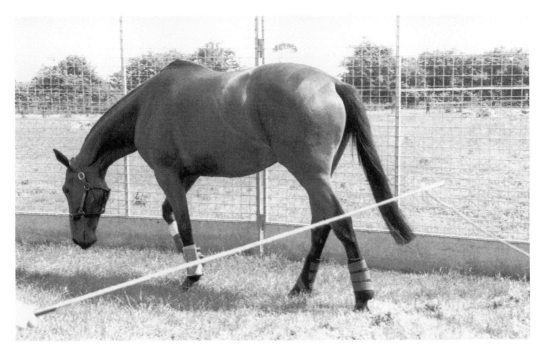

Having got him to walk, keep him going and . . .

. . . don't let him stop. Kate has relaxed so as not to set him alight again. It needs tact and practice to strike the balance between keeping him going and keeping him calm.

Kate using body language to keep Gondolier out.

He is starting to work sensibly and to listen for the words of command.

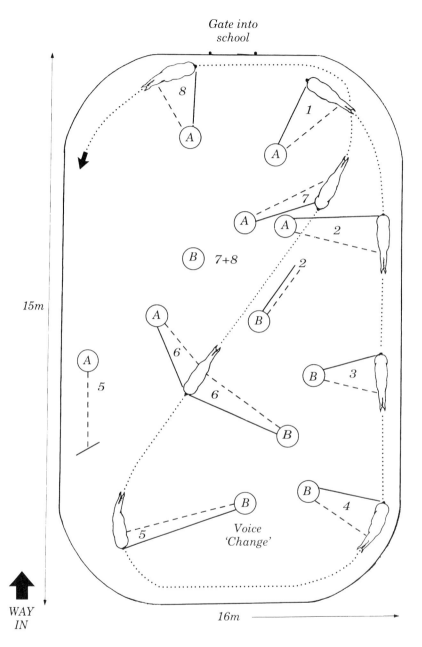

*Gate into
school*

15m

WAY
IN

16m

Changing the rein. There are two people in the school, A and B. The diagram shows in eight movements how A and B position themselves as the horse moves around the outside of the school and then changes the rein across the diagonal. The solid line drawn from the person to the horse represents the line of the whip. The broken line represents the direction of influence exerted by the person towards the horse.

Gondolier changing rein across the diagonal. He quickly learned to understand the command 'Change'. If you study the diagram opposite, you can see that he is in positions 5 and 6. Note how the two trainers use their positions and body language to teach him what is required.

off the track) – keep him going. As he starts to walk you must say 'Walk' so that he can start to associate the word and your tone of voice with his action, and if he looks as if he is stopping altogether, a commanding 'Walk on' will be needed.

Now carry on with walk and trot around the school. Use only the commands you have decided on. All the time, you are seeking for relaxation and calmness in the horse and for the horse to be increasingly attentive as he understands what it is all about. The whole art is getting your body language right to slow him down, prevent him from stopping, keep him going forward.

For the next few days concentrate on getting him working to the voice. Practice walk, trot, changes of rein at walk, stand and stand still. Don't try to make further progress until he is doing all these things calmly and without hurrying. You will find it much easier to switch him off if you turn him out for half an hour before you start and leave him out again when you have finished.

Changing the rein at trot is much more difficult than at walk so, again, don't try for those changes until he is trotting slowly enough to make enough room for himself to do it easily.

The art, as in all work with horses, is concentration. Focus. While you and he are working you must give yourself to him utterly. You will be exhausted and you will understand how quickly these new demands take their toll on his mind and body. We reward good work by getting him

He is taught 'Stand' and 'Stand still'. He must do this and then be prepared to 'Come here' (for reward) or to 'Walk on'.

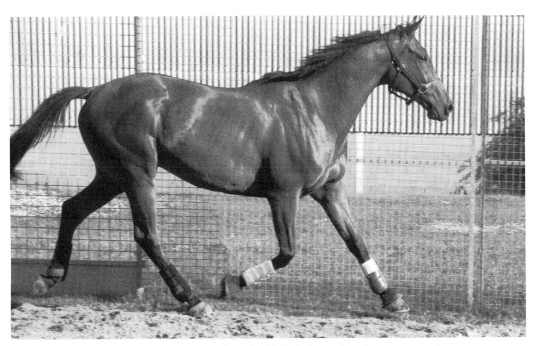

Gondolier showing a nice lengthening of stride. He is balanced and concentrated, not hurrying: a lovely example of a horse working loose.

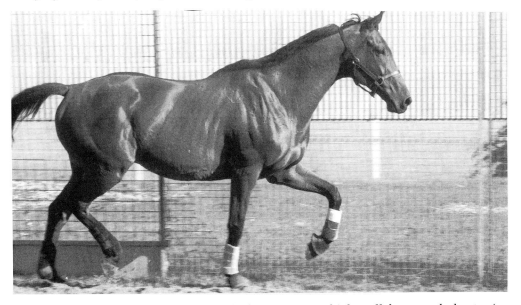

Here he is on a shorter stride. Note how the feet are coming higher off the ground: the step is shorter and, if your compare the working of the muscles with the picture above, you can see that this is harder work.

63

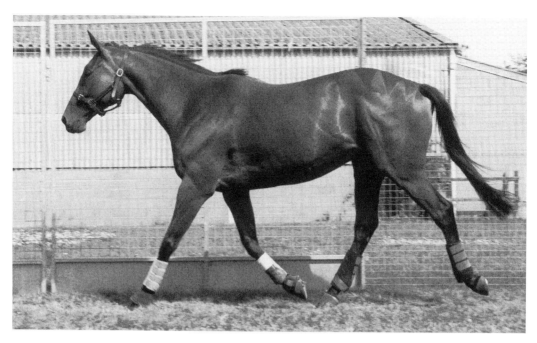

A nice, active, calm, attentive trot.

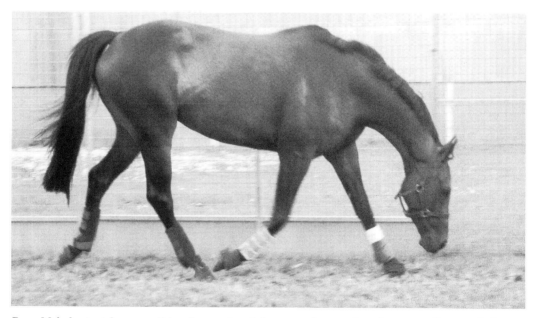

Rare Melody stretches everything forward and downward at a relaxed trot: excellent work for developing the long muscles of the neck and back. Doing this on the lunge is difficult because of the danger that a foot may get over the rein.

to 'Come here' (**after** he has stood still) and lavishing praise, affection and Polo mints on him. However, this should not happen more than three times during the exercise period or he will become greedy and lose concentration.

LENGTHENING AND SHORTENING THE STRIDE

Right through all the early training you must get your horse doing what you want without a battle. However, if his natural inclination is to turn left out of your yard, he must turn right. If, when coming home, he expects to turn in at the stable gate, he must walk on past it. And so on.

Thus, if in the loose school he tends to speed up on the long side going towards the gate and to go more slowly away from it, you must get your extension where he goes slowly and your shortening of the stride where he would prefer to hurry. And in fact this is also easier for you because

you ask for extension by encouraging him with your voice, pressing him forward with your body language and raising the point of your whip: if you do these things – even ever so gently – when he wants to run on anyway he will almost certainly break or lose his rhythm. It is easier to calm him down and tell him to go 'Slowly' there and to get him to extend his stride away from the gate.

Never go on too long. Don't forget that there is great mental effort required from him to understand and settle into this new environment and routine. And always finish on a good note. Even if you have been working for only a few minutes, if he does something really nicely, *stop* and leave it at that.

When you have got everything going as you want, you are ready for the next stage which is working over poles. But don't be in too much of a hurry – if it takes a week before you feel absolutely ready to go on, so be it.

6 Working over Poles

As in the last chapter, calmness and relaxation are what you must seek when working over poles. Even though you start with just a pole lying on the ground, don't forget that your ex-racehorse, who has worked on the flat, has probably never walked over any obstacle in his life. So a pole, particularly a painted pole, may present a problem.

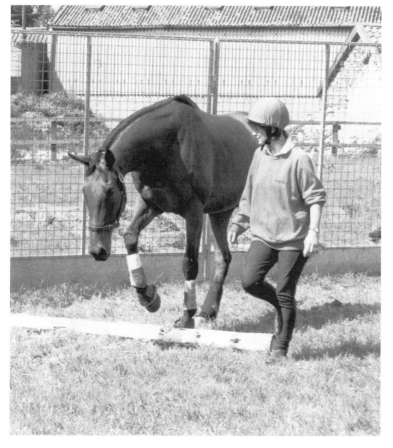

Gondolier soon learns to walk calmly over a pole. This picture demonstrates perfectly the great benefits of loose schooling. He is very relaxed and stretching forward and downward. He is learning where to step and taking care not to hit the pole, which is the first requirement of a jumper. There are no constrictions; he has perfect freedom.

Gondolier is facing a single pole placed across his track, and for the first time he is without a leader to give him moral support. This is a good example of the trainers' use of body language: Kate is leaning back so that Gondolier does not see her getting in front of him; Bizzie is further back from the track for the same reason, but is ready to take over as Gondolier approaches the pole. Kate is saying – with body and whip – 'Keep going'.

Bizzie has taken over. Gondolier starts to swing his quarters in with half a mind to turn round away from Bizzie. But Kate's whip is there to keep him at it, and Bizzie moves towards him.

Gondolier has turned half-way round; his head has come up and he is trying to avoid having to go over the pole. But the two trainers are having none of it and you can see that he is just starting to turn back. Turning round without permission is the cardinal sin: it is a refusal. This episode would certainly have cost three faults in a showjumping competition, but it was quickly corrected and Gondolier learned that he must not do it.

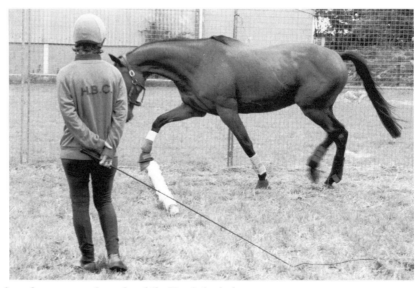

Gondolier turns back and trots over the pole while Kate's body language says, 'You're doing fine – carry on'. He is having to stretch a bit as he is a little too far away to be able to take the pole in his normal stride. But this is the result of the previous episode. The trainers now need to get him walking and crossing over the pole in his walking stride while at the same time being relaxed.

THE PURPOSE OF POLE WORK

The primary purpose of trotting over poles is to make horses look where they are going. They learn to equate their speed, distance and stride so that it becomes second nature to avoid hitting them.

This ability to measure their stride for themselves is absolutely fundamental jumping training. Horses must be able to do it naturally. It is like a kid playing with a ball in the park. When he runs up to kick the ball, he doesn't count 'Three, two, one, kick', in tune with his strides. He doesn't think about it at all. He just automatically runs up to the ball so that his feet are in the right place at the right time. It is exactly the same with a horse approaching an obstacle. We shall see, when we come to loose jumping, that the horses approaching **calmly**, unencumbered by a rider, **never** get a fence wrong. Nevertheless a young footballer needs endless practice to get his kick perfect and his approach to the ball exactly right. So, precisely, does a horse need practice, with and without a rider, to make a fault free approach and jump.

There are other advantages in working

Gondolier being inattentive and carelessly stepping on a pole. He is too fresh: we should have allowed him more time to let off steam before starting work over poles.

What a difference! He is trying really hard and making a great effort not to touch the pole. That hind leg is going to carry right through (track up). Look at the concentration on his face.

over poles such as getting them to flex their joints as they lift their feet high over the poles and to stretch their neck and back muscles as they enjoy complete freedom from interference over the obstacles. You will see this happen but don't forget the main lesson is for them to look where they are putting their feet.

INTRODUCING POLES

As with initial loose schooling, the golden rule is **Don't let him stop or turn round.**

Jumping is essentially a matter of getting from one side of an obstacle to the other so, when he walks calmly over a pole on the ground (as we hope he will), it is to all intents and purposes his first jump.

When first introducing your horse to poles, do not start the training session with a pole across his track. Work him in as you have been doing and then, towards the end of the exercise, introduce a pole or two. How quickly you advance depends entirely on his attitude.

Your horse's attitude to work over poles

Rare Melody is brilliant over poles and here she is showing herself at her best: focused, enjoying her work, absolutely accurate. Note the terrific articulation of her hocks, knees and fetlocks.

Watch Point

At every stage of your training of horses, start by briefly repeating what you achieved in the previous lesson. Do not advance to new work until you have confirmed your progress so far.

Work in the loose school is a perfect example of when that rule should be applied.

---

will give you an idea right from the start of whether you have a good jumper on your hands. Those that don't seem to mind clouting the poles are by no means such good prospects as those that pick their way carefully over them. A horse that hates knocking obstacles is likely to become a jumper of clear rounds. If you are looking for a horse for eventing or showjumping you must avoid a careless horse. Nothing is more frustrating for an event rider than everything going perfectly except that you almost always have fences down in the showjumping. In three-day-events, incidentally, your bad jumper will be at his worst after the rigours of the previous day's speed and endurance. For this reason horses known to be likely to collect many jumping penalties should never be included in teams for major championships.

You can forgive carelessness over the poles if your horse has become excited and started to dash round the school. It does happen, inevitably, but you should do your

Not like this . . .

. . . but like this. Gondolier at his best. Isn't he a fabulous mover? Here he is relaxed and concentrated, so the trainer, too, is relaxed and at ease.

This sequence of four pictures shows Gondolier walking calmly over a pole and standing still when he gets to the far end of the manège. He approaches with ears pricked; he looks intelligently forward at the pole, unruffled and confident. Kate keeps focused on him but does nothing. His mind is subconsciously calculating his stride.

He has got it absolutely right and walks over the pole with virtually no change in the rhythm of his walk. He stretches down to make sure that he is not going to touch the pole. It is the freedom from any restraint imposed by a rider that is so beneficial. This picture shows how he is learning to use his head and neck over an obstacle – the beginning of a bascule.

73

He has stayed at walk and continues to keep to the outside of the manège. Bizzie just keeps him going quietly, preparing for the halt.

best to avoid it by being patient and waiting for him to settle down before trying him over poles at all. And when you do start don't add to the poles until he is ready to accept them with equanimity. As you increase the number of poles they can all too easily become to him a confusing mass of obstacles. **Hasten Slowly.** If you ask too much, as we have all done only too often, all you do is take a great step backwards. You will have to wait all the longer before your know that he can face the poles without getting rattled. So whatever you do, don't have more than one or two poles on the ground until you are as sure as you can be that he is concentrating on his work.

Start with just one pole and let him walk over it if he will. If there is any difficulty, lead him a few times before asking him to do it on his own. Don't progress further until he is walking happily over single poles.

Thereafter you can progress – probably in one or at most two lessons – to walking over several poles, placed higgledy-

As he reaches the top of the school, Bizzie calls him to stand, while Kate has quietly moved around to make sure that he stops. Note how she places her whip to prevent him from turning in. This sequence of pictures shows what I mean when I compare loose schooling to performing a dance: trainers and horse move to a routine that the horse soon learns. As he masters it, the indications from the trainers become less and less pronounced until they can almost stand quite still in the middle of the school, making small movements when necessary, while the horse reponds to instructions given with the voice alone. What is being achieved here can be compared to the rider's objective: 'Maximum effect from minimum movement'.

piggledy around the perimeter of the school and then to trotting over two, three or four poles placed on consecutive strides. An average distance apart of about 1.3m (4ft 3in) will suit a normal stride at trot. When you have seen how your horse handles them, you can alter the distances either to make it easier and more convenient or to shorten or lengthen the stride.

THE FUNNEL

Rare Melody didn't start working over poles until Gondolier was already jumping, but she is very intelligent and loves her work so she caught up fast. She is incredibly careful and is undoubtedly going to be a real clear-round achiever – she hates to touch a pole. She hasn't such a soft and affectionate nature as

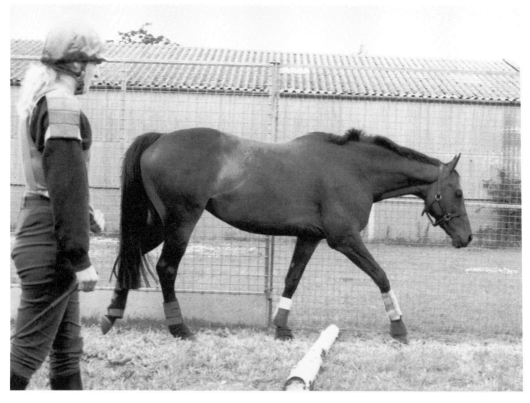

Rare Melody, walking well, is always careful not to touch the pole. Note Bizzie's position and her 'direction of influence'. Her whip is unused, but her body and movement are keeping the mare moving forward and out on the perimeter. The problem with Rare Melody is that she is a fizzy personality and is easily over-excited.

Gondolier, and when she learns (as she does very quickly) to harness that bit of cussedness that is in her nature, our guess is that she is going to be brilliant.

Gondolier, on the other hand, is not very brave and tends to become flustered if he does something wrong. When he gets unsettled he jumps on a long low trajectory, often hitting the obstacle as he does so. However, when he clouts one, he tries extremely hard next time, which is a good sign.

In order to make Gondolier jump cleaner and with a better style we formed a funnel with two poles, the ends sticking well up above the height of the first pole of a low parallel. As you can see from the pictures, the results were spectacular. He does have a beautiful jump when things go well for him.

The funnel is a wonderful schooling aid. I have never known a horse to knock this down and I must have used it a thousand times. In teaching jumpers to fold up their legs in the early stages of training there is nothing like it. See page 78.

The smaller the narrow end of the funnel, and the higher the ends above

When Gondolier gets things wrong everything tends to go haywire. Here he jumps with a long, low, flat-backed trajectory. Look at his ears and eye and you can see how worried he is. A horse like this must be taken slowly so that he finds his work easy and enjoyable.

When Gondolier gets it right he is just about perfect, as this glorious jump shows. A jump like this illustrates how much the rider must stretch forward with his hands if he is to maintain a steady contact with his horse's mouth. If training them to jump loose gets them going like this in this lovely shape, then the Royal Dublin Society has a pretty good new idea. (see Chapter 2).

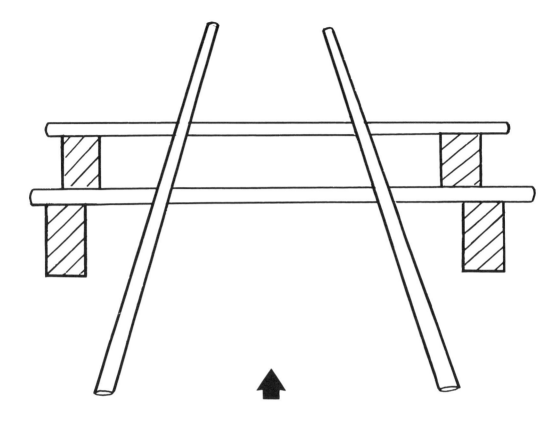

The funnel can be used over both vertical and parallel fences.

the front pole, the more it will encourage the folding of the legs. The wider it is the less daunting the fence but the easier it is to knock the pole.

We like to introduce the first jump he takes by placing it related to and after a

---

Watch Point

Use of the funnel is not permitted in the warming-up area at jumping shows.

---

trotting pole or poles. Probably the best way is to build him up to trot over three poles, then, when he is doing that well, leave a gap of about 2.75m (9ft) followed by a very small fence about 30cm (12in) in height. He may or may not bother to make an actual jump of it (See page 80), but as soon as he has got the message and is going calmly and freely over it you can proceed to make a proper jump of it, perhaps about 45cm (18in) high. As soon as he has given you one good jump – even if it is the first one he makes – lavish

Rare Melody showed from the start that she has the makings of an excellent jumper. She comes off the ground with extraordinary power from her hind legs.

Gondolier is concentrating well and finding this very easy.

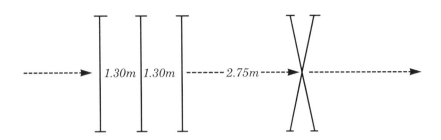

Trotting poles followed by a small fence about 30cm (7.5in) high.

You can see why we think Rare Melody is going to be a great jumper. The exercise is the one shown above. Early in her work in the loose school she always took these extravagant and exciting leaps but, although it was great fun, it was not what was wanted. Later on she became much more laid back and jumped only a little more than was needed to clear the obstacle.

praise upon him, reward him with affection and Polo mints, and **call it a day.**

Over the next few days gradually build up the jumping, going to low parallel fences as soon as you are confident that he is ready, until he is calmly and freely jumping a fence of about 1m (39in) high by 1.3m (4ft 3in) wide. The size of the fence is not important. The worst thing you can do is frighten him. Dimensions depend very much on the state of the going (footing) and the amount of space you have. It is the style of jumping and your horse's attitude to his work that really matter. Use the funnel described above. It helps enormously to get the actual configuration of the jump right. As you can see from the photographs, we got both these horses jumping really beautifully albeit over quite small obstacles and fairly simple exercises.

But we were very satisfied that we had done nothing but good with two happy, relaxed calm and stylish horses.

ASSESSING AND CONSOLIDATING PROGRESS

Before you finish the loose schooling stage of our conversion process, make sure that you are content with progress and have achieved the three objectives set at the beginning of Chapter 5:

1. To go equally well in both directions.
2. To trot over poles without hurrying the pace or hitting the poles.
3. To jump small fences in good style.

Let us consider each of these in turn:

1. To go equally well in both directions

You will have seen that the work on the flat has been both to the left and the right. Almost all horses find it easier at the beginning to go to the left – just as people are right- or left-handed by nature. The obvious response to this is to work a horse more on the rein he finds difficult, but this is wrong. The reason he finds it difficult is that it hurts: his muscles ache after a short time on the awkward rein. So start by doing more on the rein he finds easy and only gradually increase work on the other until he is equally comfortable in both directions.

This problem of one-sidedness is likely to be much more entrenched when you take on an ex-racehorse. This, I am sorry to say, is because very few trainers ever bother – even if they know how – to get their riders to rise on the correct diagonal at trot. The trouble is that it is much more comfortable to sit on the diagonal that the horse (who will prefer one diagonal to the other) finds easiest. It doesn't need Einstein to work out that the result of always coming down into the saddle on the comfortable trotting diagonal is that the horse's back becomes much stronger on one side than on the other. Any stress put on the weaker side then results in muscles clenching and going into spasm, which is obviously going to make the unfortunate animal more one-sided than ever.

Horses that are well broken are ambidextrous, but this can be and often is put to no effect when the horse goes into training. The riders always ride on the same diagonal and the horse reverts to his original preference for going one way rather than the other.

What is forgotten is that a horse that cannot gallop equally well on a left-handed or a right-handed course is at a serious disadvantage. And you can be assured that a one-sided horse has been either badly broken or badly ridden, or he has a back problem, or his teeth need attention (maybe he has a wolf tooth), or his feet are out of balance, (*see* Appendix I). **All** of these can and should be very easily cured with the result that you will have twice as good a horse.

Remember that, in a racehorse, the difference between immortality and oblivion can be as little as eighteen inches over a mile and a half. Two changes of leg because the horse is uncomfortable galloping to the left can lose you the Derby! Much was written in 1996 about the fact that all Epsom Derby winners from 1991 to 1995 ended up being sold for astronomical prices to stand at stud in Japan. But who could tell us what happened to the five horses that were second? Anything that can be done to improve performance by this tiny margin is surely well worth the effort, and although racehorses may demonstrate the point in a very dramatic way, it is true to say that any competition horse deserves similar attention in this respect: after all who ever heard of a one-sided dressage horse that did any good?

Loose schooling is a wonderful way of

An active shortened trot, the feet high off the ground, and great articulation. A pity she is swishing her tail, showing mental effort; but don't you often see this in collected work even from advanced horses.

working your horse on both reins without hurting him. Unencumbered by the weight of a rider, all his muscles work freely without interference of any kind. You can see day by day how his balance improves and how he gets around the corners ever more easily without strain or change of rhythm. The slower he goes the easier he will find it.

As you watch him improving you will see how the long muscles along the top of his neck and back develop. His outline both at rest and in his going improves: this is because he is using all his muscles correctly because he has nothing to avoid.

2. To trot over poles without hurrying the pace or hitting the poles

If, at the beginning, your horse was careless and didn't seem to mind clouting the poles, you will probably have found that as he settled down to his work and went more calmly and slowly he became increasingly successful at clearing them. At this point in his training, his steps will be higher as the easy articulation of hocks, knees and fetlocks develops.

If, on the other hand, you find that your horse has not progressed towards fluency during training and appears to be consistently clumsy and disinclined to make the

Three pictures of Gondolier jumping. Here he is at the moment of take-off, looking at the fence and concentrating on the job. (See overleaf)

Another lovely jump: Gondolier has folded his front legs well and is producing a good bascule.

The landing. His hind legs are well folded up and, as he lands, his head comes up to maintain his balance. His hind legs will come far underneath him to propel him forward in the stride after landing. Study these three pictures to work out what your hands must do to hold an even contact from the moment before take-off to the get-away after landing.

necessary effort, it is unlikely that he will turn into a good jumper.

However, before coming to this conclusion, consider whether his clumsiness may be caused by fear or confusion: satisfy yourself that you have not progressed too quickly, and so, perhaps, failed to consolidate each lesson.

3. **To jump small fences in good style**
If you have brought your horse along carefully, and if he is staying relaxed, jumping in a good style, using his head, neck and back to make a lovely bascule (parabola) over the fence; and if he is folding up both front and hind legs and not letting them dangle in the air over the fence; and if he is finding it all easy and fun; and especially if he doesn't tap the poles either as he trots over them or as he jumps them, then you are well on the way to having a first-class jumper.

But please remember that there are millions of horses, doing thousands of different jobs and it is not the end of the world if your horse is a less than perfect jumper. He may be a marvellous ride, a brilliant companion, a gorgeous mover, as brave as a tiger and perhaps, as well, adequate over fences. For such a horse there are unlimited opportunities in a career beyond the racecourse.

This picture enables you to compare a ridden horse at the moment of landing with Gondolier. Alfoxton, ridden here by Charles Coldrey, lands over the funnel exercise. Compare this with the lower picture on page 84 and you'll see the similarities. Alfoxton is folding his hind legs very well. He was a very clean jumper. (Photo. Anthony Reynolds.)

Bascule by Rare Melody.

7 Riding Away ————

When you consider that your month or so of loose schooling has done all that you want, it is time to start to riding again. Don't forget, though, that loose schooling is great fun both for your horse and for you, and in the future it is well worth while to return to it occasionally. You can both relearn these lessons and enjoy the uninhibited joys of working loose. It is, of course, especially valuable before you start riding over fences again after a prolonged period of rest. As we have explained, the muscles can be built up better and the whole body of the horse more easily used in a perfect configuration without interference.

The uninhibited joys of working loose!

By the time you decide to start riding, your horse will have had several months without a saddle or a bit in his mouth – and, if it is summer, perhaps without a rug. Your ex-racehorses will also probably never have carried any saddle other than the soft lightweight race exercise saddle or a tiny racing saddle.

Having tack on again may, therefore, be something of a surprise to him and you need to take care. At this stage we go through a mini-rebreaking exercise, which may prove to be absolutely uneventful and so, in retrospect, appear unnecessary, but it may just avoid a nasty accident.

What follows here is a basic outline of how to proceed while making sure that no one gets hurt in the process. However, if you feel you require more detailed guidance on rebreaking, please consult our first book *Breaking and Training Young Horses* (*see* Bibliography).

ROLLERING

The first thing to do is to put a roller on him. Well, actually, the first thing to do is to fit a cavesson. We take him back to his box at the end of his final exercise in the loose school. We then put on a cavesson

Rare Melody with roller and cavesson, ready for lungeing.

Here she is on the lunge with a lovely relaxed gait and carriage.

with a snaffle or a breaking bit (snaffle with keys). All the time we are taking great pains to see that he stays calm and enjoys all the attention.

Rollering is a two-person job. Leading him from a cavesson we now take him back out to the lunge ring and give him a very gentle lunge mostly at walk but with a little trot as well. Once we are sure he is settled we halt him and make him stand on the outside track with his forehand turned just into the ring. While one person (whom we'll call A) holds the front end of the horse with the lunge reins rolled and ready to go, the second person (B) puts the roller gently but firmly over the withers and lets it hang down on the far side. The breast plate is then brought round the front and buckled up. Next the girth of the roller is brought under the chest and loosely buckled up on the near side. It is then tightened just enough to stop it slipping. While this is done, the lunge whip is lying on the ground ready to be picked up straight away by B. (We are, of course, sending the horse round to the left).

Once the roller has been tightened, A now takes charge and gives the order 'Walk on', while B picks up the whip and uses it – just as was done in the loose school – to make sure the horse moves forward.

As the horse feels the roller the odds are 100–1 that nothing will happen. He has been through all this before, is perfectly used to the saddle and being ridden, is thoroughly used to both A and B training him in the loose school. He will almost certainly simply walk off on the lunge – no problem. But it is just possible that as he breathes in and feels the roller he may give a squeal and a few bucks before settling down and it was against this unlikely eventuality that we have taken all this care.

Once he has settled down with the roller and lunged calmly, especially at walk, we take him back to the stable, leaving the roller on overnight to make absolutely certain that he is thoroughly used to it again after his long break. Neither Gondolier nor Rare Melody were the least bit worried at any time during this exercise.

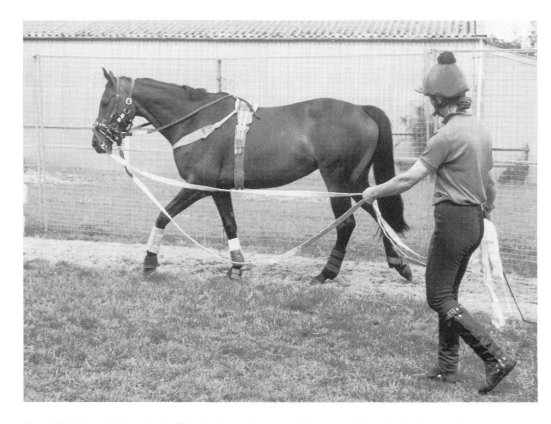

Rare Melody walking nicely. She is always interested in everything that is happening.

Annette, our lightweight rider-away, is legged up (by Catharina Sonsthagen) to lean over Rare Melody.

Watch Point

Not only do we make sure that riders **and** holders wear BHS approved safety hats, but that all riders of young horses wear body protectors at all times. Please note that it is now against the law in the UK for children under fourteen to ride in a public place without a safety hat.

GETTING ON

Next morning we can practically guarantee that you can take off the roller and put your saddle straight on. Always, though, put the bridle on before the saddle. Of course you can normally tie your horse up

(headcollar over bridle) while you saddle up, but this first time have someone standing beside his head holding him. If he is completely nonchalant about it, you can tie him up to saddle him next time.

Now the person holding him with the left hand should give you a leg up just to lean over the saddle and straight off again. Do this a few times and, if your horse is quite happy about it, stay leaning across the saddle. Hold the pommel in your left hand and use your right hand to simulate what will be your right leg when you are sitting on him. Let him feel your hand both rubbing him and gently slapping him on the neck, and where your leg will go and behind the saddle. Use your voice to soothe and praise.

91

Rare Melody trotting on the lunge. She accepted the rider without any problem at all.

Ridden away at the start of her new career. Note Emma's body language.

Above all don't be tentative. Do everything to show him that you are confident in him and in yourself. Every single thing you do during any new or reintroduced process is bonding him to you in particular and all people in general. Don't forget Xenophon's words (*see* page 29).

When you are happy get your helper to lead him around the box while you continue to lean over: talking, slapping, praising, loving him as you go. Happy so far? Put your leg over the saddle, leaning forward. Keep him going. Sit up, take up the stirrups and bingo – you are away.

If all is well, get off and lead him to your manège, lunge-ring or indoor school and repeat the process. Ride him round at walk and then at trot on both reins and when he has settled nicely and you feel it is enough, ride him back to the stable.

Next time, repeat the process in the box and, provided his back is down (i.e. he is not humping it against your weight in the saddle) have him led out of the box. Ideally you will have an old horse waiting for him who will pick up just in front of him and lead him out for a ride, preferably all on tracks and lanes and certainly not on busy roads. The role of your lead horse is terribly important in the next few days. It is:

- To set an example of calmness.
- To protect him from traffic.
- To signal traffic to slow down and if necessary stop as you go by (always acknowledge gratefully the consideration of the driver).
- To set a sensible pace at walk, trot and canter that your young horse will find easy.

Gondolier has always accepted everything with complete equanimity. Here he is going out for the first time.

For the next couple of weeks the idea is to give your horse a break from the intense mental demands we have made of him during the loose schooling period. We therefore like to spend this time just riding out – always with the lead horse – and giving him the opportunity to enjoy life in the interesting new environment of the big wide world.

Don't be in a hurry. Allow him time to have a good look at everything. Stop and talk to people you meet, sitting relaxed with a slack rein. If he looks suspiciously at something in the hedge, don't hurry past pretending it isn't there. Stop and take him up to it. Let him stretch his neck and take a few sniffs – let him realize that it is a safe place.

When you come to a grass track or field – the sort of place where he has been accustomed to canter and gallop – walk along and, with the lead horse setting an example, stop for a quiet graze. Later on you will probably want to have a canter here but it must be at a time and pace decided by you. First he must come to view it as a place that is not particularly exciting.

The work you do on made-up roads is especially valuable after a rest period.

You only have to look at Gondolier to want to ride him. Compare this picture with the one on page 48 to see how he has blossomed in the loose school.

Emma having a fine time on Gondolier. Victoria rides Persian Measure, who was in training herself and is now a very good lead horse. They are on our grass canter and Gondolier is behaving as though he had never walked on anything else. What a star!

Walking and then trotting road-work strengthens and hardens the limbs and does only good provided that the trot is **slow** and not downhill. Slow uphill trotting is a terrific strengthener and, what is more, the gentle shock at each footfall not only makes the bone harder and denser but actually thickens the cortex. You must however avoid 'the 'ammer 'ammer, 'ammer along the 'ard 'igh road', which results in splints, ringbone and side bone, and a long period out of work.

95

8 Further Training

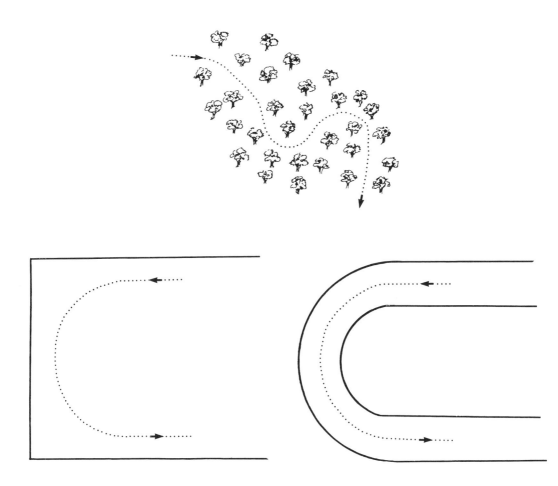

Use the same aids going round the corner on the lane or bending between trees in the wood as you would when doing the same movement in the school. Through the association of sensations your horse will learn exactly what you want from the aids that you give.

While you and your horse are out on the road again, at ease with life and enjoying it, you are preparing for the next stage of formal schooling. But first make really good use of this time to school him without his knowing that it is happening. I am talking about what we used to call the 'association of sensations'. A horse learns to associate the idea of what you want him to do with the sensation he gets from the aids that you give him. The aids we used in the loose school were the voice, the body language and the whip. The aids that you use when riding him are your legs, the weight of your body, your hands, your voice and your whip.

What we are looking for is 'the maximum effect from the minimum movement' from the rider. If you watch a good dressage horse that is really well ridden, the miraculous thing to see is how the horse appears to do everything on his own, while the rider sits, still as a mouse, apparently just allowing everything to happen without any interference whatever. And how wonderful and thrilling it is for you when you yourself establish a rapport with your horse so that you seem only to have to think what you want for him to do it. The association of sensations has become so well developed that the minutest indication from you is so well understood that your horse reacts before you have consciously moved a muscle. But don't get too depressed if you have not achieved this yet – it takes time as well as skill.

While you are riding out is the time to start. Let the terrain help you. If you have to go round a corner, which the horse is obliged to do because there are no alternatives, use the aids (legs and hands) as if you were doing the same manoeuvre in the formal environment of the school.

Trotting over poles under saddle, Rare Melody has lost none of her careful, calm but keen attitude. Note that Emma is keeping her weight right off the loins. Never do sitting trot over poles, especially on a young Thoroughbred.

97

Gondolier picks his way delicately with no danger of touching a pole.

The result of constantly repeating a signal is that your horse learns always to respond in the same way. Use the fact that he will move more strongly towards home than he will when going out. You can make use of this in your informal schooling. Make him go quietly and slowly back to the stables and walk away from them briskly. When you start doing a bit of lateral work, practise a little leg yielding on the way home when you can be sure not to kill the forward movement. But all the time, use the correct aids – especially when he is obliged to do the movement anyway – so that the aid and the movement become associated in his mind. In this way he learns all the time but without realizing that he is having lessons.

When he is settled and you are both happy riding out, take him into the school before you put him away and spend five minutes doing the things that he learned to do loose. Just walking and trotting calmly around on both reins, then over the odd pole, then over trotting poles, just as he did before. And as always: don't go on to the next stage until you are completely happy with progress so far; and make sure you finish when he has done well so that he goes back to the stable pleased with himself and with your praises ringing in his ears.

The first objective, though, is to get him hacking out calmly. This is the first stage in making him bombproof. Use the protection you get from a lead horse if it is possible. If you are on your own, try to get a friend to come over and ride out with you, at least for a few times until your horse is settled. Traffic is your main

Watch Point

Do not go into the loose school after riding out if you feel your horse is tired. Young horses are like children. You can't teach them anything if they are too fresh or too tired.

problem and it is here that your lead horse is invaluable. In this day and age it is essential that he is good in traffic. Ex-racehorses have a big advantage because in their past life most will have become used to vehicles, noise and crowds of people at an early age.

Use the land available to you to your best advantage: walk over little drains; if there is a small ditch to get over (especially if you can get a lead) use it to further his training and to make him brave; bend around trees, brush through thickets, pop over fallen branches and tree trunks; play follow-my-leader through the woods; ride down the sloping side of a disused pit or quarry; make him stand quietly while you watch something in the distance; make him walk through puddles (but only ones that are wide enough to

prevent his 'running out' around them) and so on. Seize every opportunity to widen his knowledge, increase his confidence, make him calmly accept that whatever he is asked to do is safe and is fun.

You will feel that he is growing up quickly and, before long, you can give him whole sessions in the manège. Here you must try to emulate all the exercises that he has learned to do so well loose. Follow the trotting poles by a small jump. Try to leave him unhindered by you so that he will continue to use himself over the fence in the same way as he was doing before.

And now we think we have said enough and that it is over to you to carry on using your horse for whatever career you have planned for him. Gondolier is going to be the hack for Leslie Harrison, Lord Howard

Gondolier is ready to go back to Plantation Stud. He executes this little exercise admirably. Emma is being careful to leave him with all the freedom he has been used to!

de Walden's racing manager, and his wife Ruth will school him and take him to local shows where I expect he will make a considerable impression in the dressage arena.

Rare Melody is back with Caroline Schweir and we shall be very surprised (and disappointed) if she doesn't turn into an excellent competition horse. As you have seen, she has talent to spare. She has to be treated with great tact to prevent her boiling over, but as she gets used to being good it will become a habit, and we believe that she will get better and better.

Lord Howard de Walden lent Gondolier to Chris and Vicky to be reschooled for a new career outside racing and to be used as a model for this book.

He came back looking magnificent and very much at ease with life. He was meant to come for me to ride but, since Chris had sung his praises as a potential dressage horse, my wife Ruth has pinched him. She thinks the world of him, as does her dressage instructor John Bowen.

Leslie Harrison, Plantation Stud.

Rare Melody has her ears laid back here, which is a pity. But this time she has folded up her front legs well, which, as you may have noticed, she does not always do. The funnel has been put up for her, which is the reason for this improvement.

The take-off for a good jump. She has scope to spare.

101

> A chance remark to Chris and Vicky in the village shop resulted in my recent purchase (a four-year-old mare, out of racing and with 'personality problems') being gladly entrusted into their capable hands. Chris felt his training methods would allow her true talents to emerge whilst producing a calm, confident horse. To my delight her manner and condition started to improve immediately, and it always appeared that the mare dictated the speed of progress and therefore became relaxed and happy. They retraced every aspect of her education and each experience left her growing in confidence and trust, finding the path of least resistance and the consumption of many mints!
>
> This excellent foundation has allowed me to start serious training, and I have already achieved double clears show jumping. Prior to her retraining I was beginning to doubt that the mare would be suitable to event, but now I am looking forward to the spring and our first competition. I am absolutely delighted.
>
> Caroline Schweir

When you reintroduce your horse to public events, remember that the last time he was in public was at the races; it may blow his mind somewhat. So we suggest that you take him to a little show, of any sort, and just let him see it. No entries, just let him stand around, ridden, and get bored and blasé about it. If he does get steamed up, do it again before you ask him to enter any competitions. You will know when he is ready to start by the fact that he does not get rattled by all the excitement.

One last and terribly important point. Our horses are in the world to give us pleasure. Provided we treat them properly and with affection they will always do this. No horse is too good for the job he is doing, no matter how humble, if he is content and his owner is enjoying the great happiness that is in the gift of this noble animal.

Caroline Schweir comes to collect Rare Melody. Once known as 'the lunatic', she is a reformed character. She stands quietly while her photograph is taken and, opposite, waits calmly as Caroline opens the gate, and then walks happily off down the road to her old home.

Rare Melody was placed in a dressage competition within three weeks of returning home.

The approach to a fence is the most important phase of a jump. If you take off at the right spot with the horse in the right posture nothing much can go wrong. This is a lovely approach with Rare Melody doing everything right so that Caroline is able to look at the obstacle and assess the situation with a co-operative and attentive horse.

Last Word

Here is our Tree of Classical Riding. What we have done through this book, is to take our racehorses out of the lowest branches on the right-hand side and start the process of climbing the tree towards whatever goal to which the new owner aspires. Our contention and belief is that good ex-racehorses can reach the very top of each branch and we have given actual examples of some that have done so.

Our inspiration for writing this book was the challenge presented by the controversy that was stirred up by a TV programme entitled *They shoot horses, don't they?* Our great good fortune is the never-ending supply of lovely Thoroughbreds coming out of racing every year. By using them in this way we can answer with confidence, 'No! We don't shoot horses'.

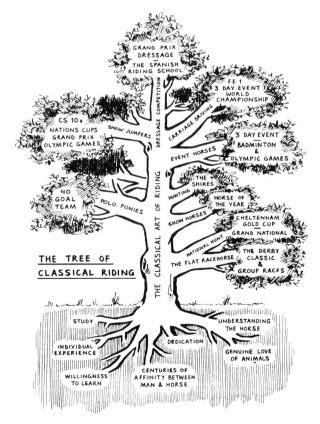

Appendix I: Look at the Feet

By Stephen Gowing A.W.C.F.

When looking at a Thoroughbred horse at a sale there are many aspects of the foot to be considered. You would be wise to remember, 'Tops will come, but bottoms never'.

These horses have been shod for fast work, which in many cases means that they have been shod short and tight. Over a period of time this can cause collapsed

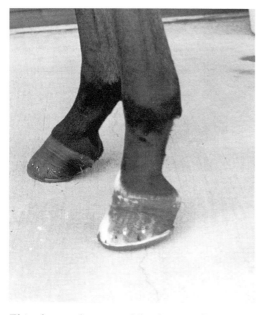

This shows what a good farrier can do even with one shoeing. If the feet had been left without expert attention, you can see from the right foot that a collapsed heel would have resulted, with dire consequences for the whole future of this good horse.

heels and the toes can become too long. Make sure that your prospective horse has a set of feet – of a pair of fronts and a pair of hinds – that fit the size of the horse: for example, a 17hh. horse must not have 10cm (4in) wide feet; rather the average width should be 13–14cm (5¼–5½in).

The hoof grows from the coronary band which should be full, round, and free from injury. The hoof itself should be a good shape with depth of heel, strong walls, the side concaved and, underneath, clear well-shaped frogs.

Good hoof – pastern axis is very important and a good farrier can help a great deal. Long toes and weak heels can also be much improved with regular shoeing. I have found bar shoes very successful: they give full support to the foot and help the heels get some depth; flat feet can also be helped with a wide web shoe with plenty of length and width at the heels, and the foot-bearing surface of the shoe slightly seated out.

If you do buy a horse with bad feet you must be prepared to spend time and money on getting them back in shape and some may need shoeing every four weeks. If you are not sure, take advice from your farrier or vet because some conditions are quite easily improved, while others will never allow the horse to be sound.

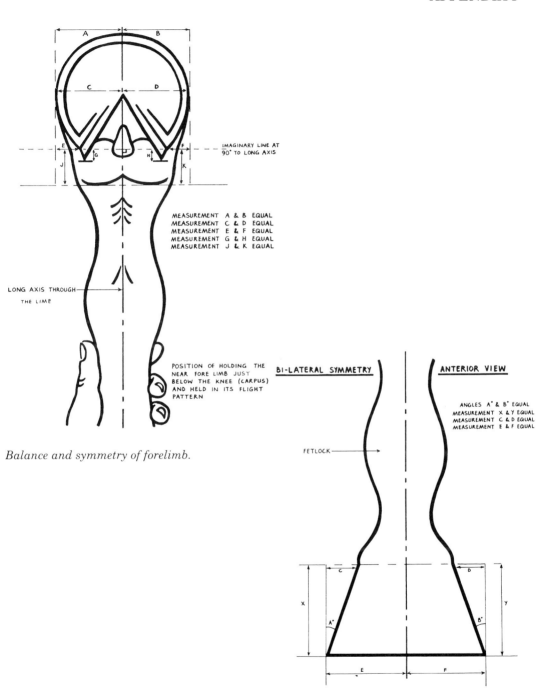

MEASUREMENT A & B EQUAL
MEASUREMENT C & D EQUAL
MEASUREMENT E & F EQUAL
MEASUREMENT G & H EQUAL
MEASUREMENT J & K EQUAL

IMAGINARY LINE AT 90° TO LONG AXIS

LONG AXIS THROUGH THE LIMB

POSITION OF HOLDING THE NEAR FORE LIMB JUST BELOW THE KNEE (CARPUS) AND HELD IN ITS FLIGHT PATTERN

Balance and symmetry of forelimb.

BI-LATERAL SYMMETRY

ANTERIOR VIEW

ANGLES A° & B° EQUAL
MEASUREMENT X & Y EQUAL
MEASUREMENT C & D EQUAL
MEASUREMENT E & F EQUAL

FETLOCK

Bilateral symmetry: anterior view.

107

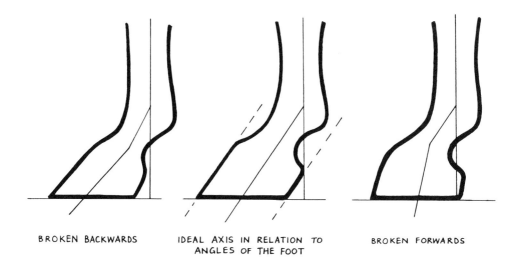

BROKEN BACKWARDS

IDEAL AXIS IN RELATION TO
ANGLES OF THE FOOT

BROKEN FORWARDS

Angles and axis.

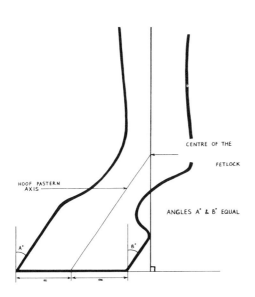

CENTRE OF THE

FETLOCK

HOOF PASTERN
AXIS

ANGLES A° & B° EQUAL

A°

B°

*Hoof balance and hoof patern axis in the ideal
forelimb: lateral view.*

Appendix II: Equine Physiotherapy
By Sarah Culverwell

The stresses placed on the Thoroughbred from the time he begins his preparation for sale, predispose his young fragile frame to mechanical imbalances. I liken the four limbs of a horse to the wheels of a car. You have one at each corner and unless they are correctly aligned so that the car (or the horse) is foursquare and goes forward absolutely straight, the result will be excessive wear and a poor performance. No vehicle (or horse) with a crooked chassis can possible give you a decent drive (or ride).

These imbalances can start in the field with boisterous play and can develop at any stage of handling through to training.

In effect the imbalance is a state in which the mechanical effectiveness of joint mobility is impaired. This is because a tiny misalignment of the joint surfaces causes a painful restriction in the natural range of movement. This has a knock-on effect through the horse's structure. If it is not caused by play, it can occur through slipping on concrete, getting cast when stabled, catching himself when first rugged, or when the process of breaking begins in earnest. There are multiple external and strong forces exerted on the young structure which, if not remedied, can create resistance from the very beginning of the animal's active life. They can

Sarah Culverwell at work.

occur through the most straightforward of exercises. For example if the horse moves on rather faster than his jockey requires the tendency is to fix one hand and give a good pull with the other. This in itself can imbalance and cause this misalignment of the tempero mandibuler joint (the jaw), which conveniently shortens to TMJ – Too Much Jockey.

If you start your working life with this imbalance through the jaw, the result will be a resistance down the neck and a consequent restriction of the shoulder movement (commonly described in competition horses as 'bridle lame'!). The restricted shoulder ricochets diagonally to impair the movement of the pelvis on the opposite side and gradually the animal loses his natural, free, swinging gait and develops a shortened and uncomfortable 'choppy stride'.

These 'gait changes' do not, to start with, show as lameness or unlevelness, and they can be felt more than seen. The imbalance causes resistances and restrictions of movement. The animal will often show his discomfort by being awkward and, perhaps, stroppy to handle. These tendencies are not, as often assumed, 'typical of a racehorse', but should be read as a message to the handler that there is a problem. These problems occur more frequently in young horses but, luckily, are more easy to cure than they are in older, more mature bodies.

Corrective measures are best taken as early in the horse's new career as possible to ensure that the whole horse can benefit from his change of environment. It is in any case always horrible for any athlete to work under the stress of pain: activity becomes a misery and, by trying to avoid pain, easy movement and rhythm are lost. This can so impair a horse's performance

that he may be written off as useless when in fact he is potentially a star waiting to be discovered.

If the horse is in discomfort, and perhaps in positive pain caused by imbalances in his structure (and in turn causing a crooked chassis), he will not thrive as one would expect; he will certainly not be able to develop a muscular posture that enables him to work correctly and give a true outline. For this reason it is highly desirable that you ask your physiotherapist to give him a good check-over as a part of the health check-up and 'service' before the turning-out period.

Tight muscles in the horse's back are a primary indication of an alignment imbalance along with a poor development of the main extension muscles of the quarters (the hamstring, *Biceps femoris*).

The tight back muscles are symptomatic of the problem, the cause of which comes from misalignment of the four corners of the animal's structure. It is obvious that a frame that is out of line is going to twist and so injure the horse's back. Our job as physiotherapists is first to release the tightness (spasm) along the neck and back, and then to get the foursquare alignment right which will allow the horse to develop his so far hidden potential.

Methods of mobilization and occasional manipulation free up the tensions present. It is hugely rewarding to see the tension release, even while the treatment is administered. The next step is to allow the animal to accept psychologically that there has been a mechanical alteration and that there is no more pain. When that happens he will know that he can be brave enough to let down and stride out with a new confidence.

Bibliography

Coldrey, Capt. C. and V., *Breaking and Training Young Horses*, The Crowood Press (1990).

Milner, Mordaunt, *The Godolphin Arabian: The Story of the Matchem Line*, J.A. Allen & Co. (1990).

Willett, Peter, *The Classic Racehorse*, Stanley Paul (1981).

Xenophon, *The Art of Horsemanship*, c. 430 BC.

Index